PRESS
PLAY

PRESS PLAY

▶

A Teenager's Guide to Living an AWESOME LIFE

LINDA BONNAR

THE
DREAMWORK
COLLECTIVE

This edition was published by The Dreamwork Collective
The Dreamwork Collective LLC, Dubai, United Arab Emirates
thedreamworkcollective.com
Printed and bound in the United Arab Emirates
Cover Design: Stephanie Hannus

Copyright © Linda Bonnar, 2017, 2019

ISBN 978-0578-50-547-3
Approved by National Media Council
Dubai, United Arab Emirates
1788669

All rights reserved. No part of this publication may be reproduced, stored, or transmitted in any form or by any means, electronic, mechanical, photo-copying, recording, or otherwise, without prior permission of the publishers. The right of Linda Bonnar to be identified as the author of this work has been asserted and protected under the UAE Copyright and Authorship Protection Law No. 7.

Press Play has been written to encourage, coach, motivate and guide, teenagers to make changes in their lives and be more successful in relation to the subjects discussed specifically within the book. This book is not designed to replace, nor should it be used instead of, specific professional medical (including psychological or psychiatric) advice. For diagnosis of specific medical, psychological, psychiatric or educational learning difficulties, please consult a relevant professional in these specific fields. The publisher and the author are not responsible for any professional help that any reader engaging in this book may choose to pursue as a result of following the information given in this book. The references given are for informational purposes only and the author and publisher would like to make the reader aware that these websites may have changed since the printing of this book.

Contents

Introduction ... 9
How to Use this Book ... 13

Part 1: Personal ... 15

The challenges we deal with:

1. I hate the way I look ... 16
2. I'm constantly thinking the worst about situations ... 21
3. I just cannot get motivated to do anything ... 33
4. Goal setting: How do I even do it? ... 39
5. Everything is up in the air for me right now, and I've no idea where to even begin to sort it out ... 45
6. Surely there's a one-stop formula to overcome the challenges I'm facing? Or is that positive thinking? ... 52
7. I worry all the time, about everything ... 59
8. I get anxious about the little things to the point where it makes me feel sick ... 59
9. I'm totally stressing about life in general ... 69
10. I go on social media a lot, but I notice that it only seems to make me feel worse about myself ... 81

Part 2: Friends ... 89

The challenges we deal with:

11. I feel like I don't have many friends/I would like more friends ... 91
12. I don't like going to parties, but then I feel left out when it's all my friends talk about ... 96
13. Compared to my friends, I feel fat and unattractive. I've started dieting but can't seem to stop ... 101
14. I feel my friends don't care about me anymore ... 105
15. I'm concerned that my friend might be depressed, and I don't know what to do ... 108
16. My friend is in a toxic and abusive relationship ... 113
17. I'm not sure if I'm jealous or envious of my friends, but either way, it's not a nice feeling. How can I stop it? ... 118
18. My friends think I'm really shy, when in fact I'm terrified I'll say the wrong thing to someone I've just met ... 123
19. I feel pressured into doing things in my friendship group that I'm just not comfortable with ... 128
20. My friends have started to comment on my temper. I just can't seem to control it. I think I've got anger management issues ... 132

Part 3: School ... 139

The challenges we deal with:

21. I just can't seem to focus at school ... 140
22. I'm not getting good grades and my parents aren't happy about it ... 140
23. I can't get motivated to study ... 148
24. I don't know how to study! ... 152
25. I feel like my teachers hate me, so I can't be bothered doing any work for them ... 158
26. I find it really difficult to get organized for school every day; I need help getting organized ... 163
27. I really want the confidence to speak in public, but it terrifies me ... 169
28. I made a mistake a few years ago, and now I'm labelled at school for it ... 174

29. All this talk of interviews is freaking me out; I've no idea what to do in them . . . 179
30. I'm being bullied and it's making my life hell . . . 183

Part 4: Family . . . 191

The challenges we deal with:
31. There's loads of pressure on me to study something I'm just not interested in . . . 193
32. There are never conversations; it's always confrontations . . . 199
33. It's those same twenty questions when I get in the car every day . . . 204
34. I feel like I'm compared to my siblings all the time and I hate it . . . 208
35. I'm leaving for university next year, but my parents still treat me like I'm twelve . . . 214
36. My parents don't allow me to go out and all my friends are allowed out . . . 220
37. My parents keep asking me what I'm going to do after school and I have no idea . . . 225
38. I feel like I'm not being true to myself or true to my family, and it eats me up inside . . . 232
39. I'm fed up living away from my real home. We get shipped around a lot with my parents' work . . . 236
40. I'm worried my parents are going to get divorced . . . 243

Epilogue . . . 247
Notes . . . 249
Acknowledgements . . . 251
About the Author . . . 253
About the Publisher . . . 255

Introduction

If you are a teenager, if you have teenagers, if you work with teenagers, this book is for you.

When I was working as a teacher, I realised how tough it was being a teenager, and I felt like it was actually getting tougher. Apart from the pressure at school, there was everything that went on outside of the classroom, too: friends, families, body image, social media, stress . . . Sure, some students were sailing through, but many others were struggling. As their teacher, I knew I was there to get them the best grades possible, but I knew there was so much more they needed.

Our world is a truly wonderful place to be in right now in so many ways, but there are also things about today's society that I just can't bear to think about either. There is a great deal of uncertainty around what the future job market will look like, and so many well-meaning adults put huge amounts of pressure on their teenagers in order to try and equip them for a competitive workplace. Doing your best is no longer good enough: now some parents and teachers expect students to not just work hard, but to excel in all areas of their lives. "Become an all-round student," we tell them. "Join the debating club, volunteer for charity services, be a sports star, play the piano, and of course, get that top grade in math, too!" And then there's the pressure of social media, where it's important to look fabulous at all times, because who knows what photos you might be tagged in? Be available all the time. Don't stand out, make sure you fit in. Pressure? What pressure?

This book addresses forty of the most prevalent real-life issues teenagers are facing today and offers a range of coaching skills, tools, and techniques to overcome these issues successfully and move forward confidently in life. Issues such as body image, self-confidence, stress, anxiety, organization, study skills, interview techniques and having "tough conversations" are all topics that have been raised by my coaching clients and are dealt with in four main sections: Personal, Friends, School, and Family.

This book is for you if you're doing well but want to be doing better. This book is for you if you're not doing great and you're not sure what to do about it. If you're interested in learning how to manage your emotions and reactions better, this book is for you. If you're keen to develop a greater understanding of mind-management and relationships, or if you're seeking stress-management techniques, this book is for you. This book is for you if you've got a family, regardless of whether it is a slightly annoying family or a great family! This book is for you if you're finding school tough, or if you'd just like to get on top of things. This book is for you if you're not a young person, but you'd like to understand them a bit better. This book is for you if you'd just like to gain a bit more control in your life.

The timing of this book couldn't be better. At the time of writing this edition, the world population is 7.6 billion. The internet has 4.2 billion users; 3.03 billion social media users with the average user having (on average) 5.45 social media accounts. Articles on the "Compare and Despair Syndrome" continue to flood the media; there is a real fear that social media negatively impacts our young people's mental health. *Press Play* will equip you with skills to handle problems, tools to deal with stress, and techniques to build stronger relationships.

Press Play is honest. In this book I share my own story with you. I know that these tools and skills work because they are all changes that have helped me get to where I am now. *Press Play* is realistic. There are other books out there for you that seem to think we all live in la la land—just think positively and everything will be okay. But the reality is that that's not how it works. Yes, thinking positively is helpful, but it must be accompanied by consistent constructive action, too. There's no magic formula, but if you want to get different results in your life, this book will help you get that.

For years as a teenager, I knew I had issues—quite a few of them. I had developed such low self-esteem and a dangerous desire for perfection in all areas of my life that by the time I was twenty-one, I was diagnosed with an eating disorder, an anxiety disorder and depression. And even after this diagnosis, it still took me years to develop the strength and courage to get the help I actually needed. I knew I needed help, but the problem was that I had no idea where to start and I had no idea how to make the changes I needed to. And here's the thing about creating change in our lives: we need to want to change, we need to know what to change, and we need to know how to change. When we don't have one of these pieces, we get stuck.

Throughout my twenties, I saw psychologists, psychiatrists, and nutritionists to help me overcome these issues, and while they were all helpful in their own way, I still felt I needed something more; I needed to be able to take greater control of my life and move myself forward. I was talking about it with a friend one day and she recommended I consider doing a Neuro-linguistic Programming (NLP) Coaching course. I had heard of NLP and coaching but didn't know too much about it and honestly questioned its ability to help me. I couldn't have been more wrong.

Despite what some people think, coaching is not about giving advice at all. A coach is not a psychiatrist, psychologist, or medical professional. Coaching and NLP Coaching are about empowering people with the resources they need to move forward in life, to support them on their road to absolute brilliance. I believe that everybody has the ability to be amazing, and I believe that everybody has the resources they need to succeed; sometimes we just need some help along the way.

I wrote this book for those very reasons: to support, guide, motivate, and empower you to take the driving seat and become the driver of your own success. Welcome to your coaching book, *Press Play*. I hope you find it useful.

How To Use This Book

When I started this book, I was adamant that it was going to be all about YOU and empowering YOU. So instead of just telling stories, I've divided the book into four main parts: Personal, Friends, School, and Family. Within each part, I have identified the issues highlighted from my research and offered a range of skills, tools, and techniques to enable you to begin to deal with these challenges and move forward confidently. The whole book revolves around taking action. One of the most effective first steps you can take with any issue is to get it out of your head and onto paper, so the book I've created has space for you to do just that. You'll notice the little pause, rewind, fast-forward, and play icons I've used throughout the book to encourage you to.

⏸ Pause to think about the issue or reflect on it.

⏪ Rewind and put yourself back in a particular situation to get a better perspective on it.

⏩ Fast-forward and consider when you can use this in the future.

▶ Lastly, the play icon, which is there throughout the book to encourage you to Press Play and take action now!

This book does not claim to have all the answers. It is designed to help you make better choices, and to help you move on from the ones that haven't been so great. You may find that not all of the issues are completely applicable to you right now, which I fully understand, but simply reading about the issues other teenagers are experiencing will help you to develop a greater awareness of others, and a greater level of empathy, which is always a great thing. This book will hopefully be an entertaining read, too! I poke fun at myself and the way my crazy world works, because learning to laugh at yourself is very empowering.

Now let's dive into learning the skills and tools you need to take action and advance with confidence in all areas of your life.

Linda

Personal

The Challenges Dealt With In PART 1

1. I hate the way I look.
2. I'm constantly thinking the worst about situations.
3. I just cannot get motivated to do anything.
4. Goal setting: How do I even do it?
5. Everything is up in the air for me right now, and I've no idea where even to begin to sort it out.
6. Surely there's a one-stop-formula to overcome the challenges I'm facing? Or is that positive thinking?
7. I worry all the time, about everything.
8. I get anxious about the little things to the point where it makes me feel sick.
9. I'm totally stressing about life in general.
10. I go on social media a lot, but I notice that it only seems to make me feel worse about myself.

1 I hate the way I look.

If I had a dollar for every time I've heard someone say this to me, or I've said it myself, then I'd have the penthouse in New York I saw advertised this summer for $26 million! And while I've learned to live with how I look, for anyone reading this who is thinking the title is referring to them, I know exactly how you feel. Here's the thing about your body—it's yours, and you've got to live in it. It can be as wonderful and amazing as you want it to be, and you can reward it continuously, or you can treat it like a dump, continue to punish it, and see how it rewards you in return. It won't.

Step one is you must learn to love your body. It took me a long time to learn this. When I stood in front of the mirror, I hated what I saw, and so at the age of twelve, I made the decision to go on my first diet. Little did I know this diet would become a way of life for me, and something that would consume me. Did my diet get me closer to looking like supermodel Gisele Bündchen? No. Did it make me happier? Hell no!

I used to hate my legs so much. I thought they were too short. I would stand in front of the mirror asking, "Why are they not thinner?", Or "What is going on with my thighs?" And now? Now, I'm reminded that these are the legs that help me run marathons and ultra-marathons, they are the legs that keep me on my horse, they are the legs that remind me how far I've come in life, and they're pretty awesome!

Now this change of mindset about my body didn't happen overnight, and I'm not going to tell you that it will happen overnight for you either, because changing your mindset takes time, practice, patience, and above all—consistency. I have worked with people before who seem to expect me to wave my magic wand and sort their problems out! But unfortunately, I don't have that magic wand, and anyway, how much you change will depend on YOU and how much YOU work for it. So, as we go through this book, please keep in mind that for change to come about, we've got to be patient and consistent. Your mind is an incredibly powerful tool; learn to control it, or it will control you.

Let's begin by taking some action. It's easier said than done, I get that. Remember that all new habits are formed with baby-steps. The first thing I want you to do is to begin to reframe how you see your body, how you view it, and how you feel about it. I used the following steps as my own starting points to develop a more positive body image too, and I cannot recommend them enough.

STEP 1: Every morning when you wake up, I want you to write down one thing that you love about your body or about yourself. I don't care if it's something like, *Oh, my eyebrows are fab today,* or *I'm a kind person,* but you must find something you love about yourself and you must write it down. (You can use the Big I, little i image at the end of this chapter to help you with this task.) Of course you can add as many things as you like to your list, it doesn't have to be just one—the more you can add from the beginning the better.

STEP 2: After one week of completing this morning task, I want you to stand in front of a mirror and read aloud all the things you've written so far back to yourself. As you read through your fantastic list, remember to stand tall and proud with a smile on your face; proud of all the things your body can do and proud of all the things you love about your body and yourself.

When we take consistent action to create change, change happens. I promise that the negative thoughts you currently have about your body will change, but nobody else can do this for you, only you.

The reality is that there are very few people who will honestly tell you that they are completely happy with the way that they look. But for every insult you throw at your body, there will be somebody ready to compliment it—trust me. Is there anything else you can do? Oh, an extension task for you eager beavers! You can always fake it too, of course, and the following quick trick is great for anyone who's not very comfortable socially.

I'm not a huge fan of meeting new people. I've learned to love it because of my work, but years ago, I dreaded it. I always felt uncomfortable and thought *What if people are looking at me and I look like a right mess?* or *What if they think I don't fit in here? What if?*

The reality is that people don't really care about me that much. I don't mean that in a "no-one cares about me" way, I mean it literally. People don't care about me that much because they are too busy worrying about themselves. And even if they think I do look a right mess, they'll get over it.

▶ What do I do now? I use part of the Superwoman Pose when I'm in public. I push my shoulders back, I hold my head high as if someone is pulling me up on a string, I smile, and walk forward. I'm often terrified inside, but no one knows that from looking at me, so I fake it. It works! The smile is the key here, because if you don't smile you can look like a hired assassin. Smile when you enter a room, it relaxes people and makes you look amazing, too. To build my self-confidence a little more before I deliver a speech on stage or something, I practice the full Superwoman Pose by standing with my feet hip-distance apart and placing my hands on my hips like I'm Wonder Woman! Now give it a go for yourself. Taking on this more positive posture will encourage more positive feelings and you'll look more confident instantly.

Big I, little i.

I Am...

I've chosen to put this Big I little i task in between these two specific chapters because I feel it's pertinent to both. The whole point of this task is to fill this "Big I" with all the smaller things that you like and love about yourself. Feel free to use this one, but I recommend making yourself your own "Big I" on a large piece of paper so you can work on it. Every morning as soon as you get out of bed, your task is to fill in at least one new thing on this chart. Keep reading over what you've already written to remind yourself how well you're doing! You can include anything in this, anything that's relevant to you. So what are you made up of? Are you funny? Punctual? Honest? A good friend? Kind? Educated? Sporty? Musical? Creative?

> Self-confidence is the most attractive quality a person can have. How can anyone else see how awesome you are if you don't see if yourself?

KEY TAKEAWAYS FROM THIS CHAPTER:

❶

If you focus on what you don't like about your body, that's all you'll see. Instead, remind yourself of all the amazing things your body can do.

❷

Use the Superman/Superwoman pose to fake a bit of confidence when you need it, because when we change our posture or stance, we can change how we feel inside.

❸

Look at yourself in a mirror, smile, and say three nice things about yourself.

> *"Your body hears everything your mind says."*
> — NAOMI JUDD

2 I'm constantly thinking the worst about situations.

As a life coach, I'm always working with people to make changes in their lives. Quite often my clients will immediately look for external things in their lives to change, such as how they spend their time or what they eat, when the best place to start is internally, with your thoughts. Let me share a quick story that relates to this. When I was working as a teacher, I got an email one day from my principal: "Linda, come and see me when you have a minute, please." Nothing else, just that one sentence. Immediately my head started racing at about one hundred miles an hour, and in the space of about thirty seconds I had predicted that my principal was about to fire me! The racing thoughts continued with *I'll have to move home to Ireland and live with my parents*. (Yes, somewhere along that train of thought I had created a story that my husband had left me, too.) I start thinking about selling my stuff, packing up, *What shipping company should I use? Will I get all my salary if I have to leave now?* And yes, before I knew it, I had blown the whole thing out of proportion and neglected the pile of marking I was meant to be doing. Did I get fired? No. Was allowing the negative cycle of thoughts in my head to continue a good use of my time and energy? Absolutely not.

Experts reckon we have between fifty thousand and seventy thousand thoughts a day. Personally, I think some of us have more. Of course, realistically they're not all going to be positive and about the sunshine, are they? You CANNOT control every single thought that pops into your head, but what you can do is gain control over your reactions to certain thoughts. This whole idea of mind management begins with your thoughts so we're going to work through a series of thinking errors and look at what we can do to deal with them in a more constructive way.

I was first introduced to the process of tackling thinking errors when I started seeking help for depression and an eating disorder. At the time, I knew that my thinking wasn't rational. I knew it wasn't "normal" as such, but for me, my way of thinking had become the norm. If you've had a particular style of thinking for a period of time, especially for years like I did, that's not going to change overnight. It can be incredibly frustrating and cause increasing anxiety until you decide to deal with it. The first piece of advice I'm giving you in this section is to get things out of your head and onto paper. Write it down. Then share it.

Find someone you can share your demons with; it could be a friend, a family member, a teacher. It might need to be a medical professional, and that's perfectly fine.

Once I had plucked up the courage to speak about the type of thoughts I was having, and once I started to tackle my thinking errors, it was like this huge weight was lifted off my shoulders. Granted, I often felt very stupid about the types of thoughts I was having, but I also knew that I had to change them because they prevented me from living the kind of life I wanted. My thoughts were so erroneous they reduced my quality of life. They kept me away from social situations, they kept me weak, and they prevented me from taking risks and from being more successful. My thoughts were the things that kept me in that metaphorical straitjacket because they destroyed my ability to make good choices. I knew things had to change.

The following thinking errors were things that I first had to deal with when I started getting help for my own issues. They're based on CBT (Cognitive Behavioural Therapy) and taken from the work I did with my doctor. It's an incredibly powerful tool. This stuff is like gold to me, and years later I'm still using it on myself. The thing about these negative thoughts is that they usually don't come alone; they travel in packs and can quickly spiral, forming a vicious circle. Below is an example to show this more clearly.

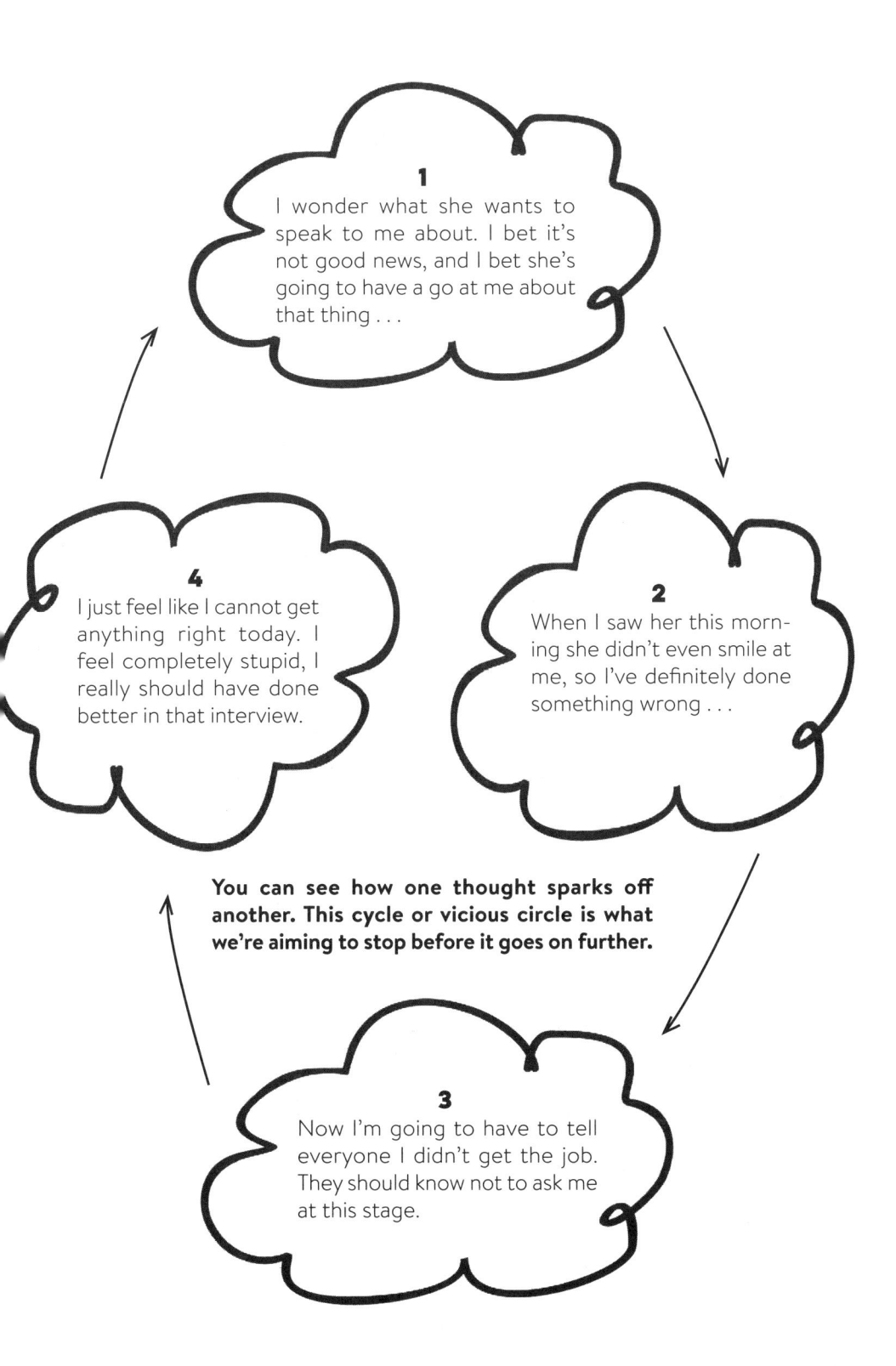

1
I wonder what she wants to speak to me about. I bet it's not good news, and I bet she's going to have a go at me about that thing . . .

2
When I saw her this morning she didn't even smile at me, so I've definitely done something wrong . . .

3
Now I'm going to have to tell everyone I didn't get the job. They should know not to ask me at this stage.

4
I just feel like I cannot get anything right today. I feel completely stupid, I really should have done better in that interview.

You can see how one thought sparks off another. This cycle or vicious circle is what we're aiming to stop before it goes on further.

⏸️ We call these series of thoughts Automatic Negative Thoughts, or let's call them ANTs for short. Our aim here is to:

1. Recognize the ANT that's taking place
2. Label it
3. Stop yourself and ask *Have I got evidence to support this thought?* Consider *What is a more constructive thought I can have?*

We want to replace these ANTs with CATs—Constructive Automatic Thoughts. It may sound like a whole separate job to do, but remember we're working on mind management here—breaking old habits and building new ones—and this takes time, patience, and consistency.

There tend to be about ten main thinking errors, or cognitive distortions. Let's take a closer look at each one, so we know what we are dealing with.

1. **Catastrophizing:** Blowing things out of proportion, as we saw in the example above. *This is the worst day of my life.*
2. **Double Standards:** When it's okay for you but not okay for someone else, or vice versa. *It's fine that Laura didn't pass her exam, but if that happened to me, I'd die*, or *It's okay for me to flirt with someone else, but if my girlfriend did that, I would not be impressed.*
3. **Mind Reading:** Imagining you know what someone is thinking. *I know she's mad at me because she didn't say hello to me this morning.*
4. **All-or-Nothing/Black-and-White Thinking:** Literally only looking at the event in extremes and ignoring the shades of grey. *There was nothing good about my holiday, absolutely nothing.*
5. **Labelling:** Judging people based on their behaviour. *I locked my keys in the car; I'm so stupid*, or *She's such a loser.* Let's label jars, and not people.
6. **Unrealistic Expectations:** Identified by "should", "must", and "have to". It's when we place our set of rules onto ourselves or someone else and expect them to be carried out. Unrealistic expectations are a huge cause of guilt and frustration. *I have to go to the gym every day*, or *He should know what I mean about this.*
7. **Overgeneralizing:** When we select one negative aspect of a situation and apply it across the board. *I got a C in my calculus exam; I can't do math.* We

might even expect it to happen again as we presume it's part of a pattern and not a one-off occurrence.
8. **Personalization:** The idea that things others say or do is a direct attack on us personally. Or it can also refer to comparisons we make between ourselves and others. *Gina is in a bad mood, I must have done something to upset her.*
9. **The Reward Fallacy:** The idea that our good deeds and sacrifices have to pay off. We then get frustrated when this doesn't happen. *I'm a good person; this shouldn't happen to me.*
10. **Blaming:** As it is! Blaming others for how we feel. *She makes me feel really stupid.* As Eleanor Roosevelt said, "No-one can make you feel inferior without your consent".

Now that you have an understanding of these thinking errors, have a go at completing the table on the next page. Remember, not all of these may apply to you. You may find two of them apply or you may find all of them apply—it doesn't matter! Our focus is on constructing more useful ways of thinking.

▶ In the first blank column of the table on the following page, I want you to think about a time when you've experienced this particular distortion or ANT in your thinking. If it's a common one, you might write down, "every time Mum shouts at me", or whatever applies to YOU. In the second blank column, have a go at identifying a more constructive thought (CAT) to replace the ANT.

The Thinking Error	When I'm likely to experience this/ When I do experience this . . .	A more constructive thought to have/A more useful reaction to this type of thought could be . . .
Catastrophizing		
Double Standards		
Mind Reading		
All-or-Nothing/ Black-and-White		
Labelling		
Unrealistic Expectations		
Overgeneralization		
Personalization		
The Reward Fallacy		
Blaming		

⏸ Did the exercise help you to notice any particular triggers?

⏸ The biggest way to combat any of these thinking errors is to check for evidence, and we do this by developing the habit of asking ourselves better questions. A key takeaway here is that instead of asking yourself *Why has this happened to me?*, get into the habit of asking more "how" and "what" questions. Of course, there is a time and a place for "why" questions, and I'm not telling you to remove them from your language altogether. However, I have found, and continue to find, that asking "Why?" can open up a whole Pandora's box of excuses, and nobody wants to hear excuses, do they? Think of when your teacher has asked you **why** you haven't met the deadline or **why** your homework isn't done. "Why" questions can also lead you into a negative circle of questioning and make you defensive, which is when the list of excuses then pops up.

As a teacher, I learned to ask my students better questions like "When will I have the homework?" or "What's got to happen in order for you to have this on my desk in the morning?" I've moved on from the fact the work isn't done and on to how we can actually get it done. You need to do the same with your thinking. Move on from an unpleasant experience by getting rid of the *Why me?* and introducing the *What do I need to do now?* or *How can I learn from this?* or *Do I have someone who can help me with this?* It's not about ignoring our mistakes. It's about learning from your experiences. It is always about checking the evidence, learning, and growing. So, in learning to check for evidence, on the next couple of pages are examples to help you with the previous activity.

The Thinking Error	ANT	CAT	Reality Of It All
Catastrophizing	This is the worst day of my life. I'm never going to get into university if I can't pass a simple math test.	I've gotten through math problems before, and I'll get through them again.	When we catastrophize, we tend to blow the problem out of proportion. Instead, we need to look at the problem rationally.
Double Standards	If my friends don't do well in the test today, that's okay for them, but it's not okay for me. I have to get full marks today.	How do I think it's different for me? Why would the same standards not apply to everyone? Is that fair?	It's not one rule for you and another rule for someone else. If it's okay for your friend to get a certain result in a test; it's okay for you, too.
Mind Reading	I know she doesn't like me; she walked past me in the corridor without saying anything.	How do I know? Could there be any other possible reason for her not saying hello to me this morning?	If you're worried someone is upset about something you've said, then ask them. And remember not everyone will like you either.
All-or-Nothing/ Black-and-White Thinking	I literally cannot find anything positive about this test I just got back—nothing.	Did I make any improvements since last time? Even in extending my answers anywhere? Did I use the feedback I was given? What do I need to change? Who can I ask?	Sometimes we need a fresh perspective to look at things. What might appear to be a "failure" at first might not be one at all. Things are not always purely black or white, and it's our job to look for the shades of grey that exist. Progress, not perfection, remember!

The Thinking Error	ANT	CAT	Reality Of It All
Labelling	This is typical. I'm so stupid. I can't believe I failed my driving test.	I need to take the feedback from today and use it to help me. What did I do well today? What do I need to work on for my next test?	Learn to use setbacks as opportunities to learn more, and to become better. See them as things to become more aware of.
Unrealistic Expectations	I can't believe my parents got me this for my birthday! They should know I'm no longer into this kind of stuff.	Have I actually communicated my new tastes and interests with my parents? How are they supposed to magically know if I don't tell them?	To this day, I've never met a mind reader. Sometimes even after telling someone something five hundred times, they still won't remember because it's just not that important to them—and that's okay.
Overgeneralizing	I mess up every relationship I get into.	Where's the evidence to support the thought that I've messed up EVERY relationship I get into?	Sure, we might have made some poor choices in our previous relationships, everybody does. It's what we learn from these experiences that matter.
Personalization	I must have said something to upset him. I wonder what it was. Was it that thing from last year?	I'm going to ask Tom if everything is okay. He could just be having a bad day.	Not everything revolves around us!

The Thinking Error	ANT	CAT	Reality Of It All
Personalization /Comparison	I hate that they are just so perfect at sports all the time! Why can't I be like that?	If I want to get better at running, what steps could I take? It's great for them they're so sporty. I admire their dedication.	Stop comparing yourself to others and focus on your own path.
The Reward Fallacy	I'm a good person; I deserve to have this go right for me.	Whatever happens as a result of this, I know I have the resources to handle it.	Sometimes life is just not fair, and this is a much more useful thought to carry around.
Blaming	This is all Dad's fault; he makes me feel so inferior to the others sometimes, he just drives me crazy!	What's a better way for me to deal with what Dad has just said to me? Getting angry doesn't help me at all.	No-one can drive you crazy unless you give them the keys! Stop blaming people and take back control.

Now it's over to you. What things in particular stood out for you in this chapter?

Sometimes people think making change is about just stopping something *or* just starting something else, when in fact we often need to do both. To help you gain even greater control over your thoughts, identify three things you will stop doing and three things you will start doing to manage your thoughts better.

STOP:
1.
2.
3.

START:
1.
2.
3.

I'm all about accountability with my clients. So, it's important that you take responsibility for this work you are undertaking. Set yourself a date in which you will review the above goals and see how well you have done so far.

I highly recommend writing your list of STOP and START thinking goals somewhere that you will see them on a daily basis. You could journal or even blog your progress. Remind yourself of these things every day, and they'll become second nature to you and help you to build new and better habits. Don't forget to reward yourself for your efforts too!

KEY TAKEAWAYS FROM THIS CHAPTER:

❶

Your thoughts are so powerful, they control your feelings. By controlling your thoughts, you can change your behaviours and then change your life.

❷

Remember, feelings are not facts. Challenge your negative thoughts by checking for factual evidence.

❸

Stop asking yourself "why" questions and start asking yourself more solution-focused questions like *What evidence do I have to support this thought?* or *How can I handle this in a more constructive way?*

> *"I don't fix problems. I fix my thinking. Then problems fix themselves."*
>
> — LOUISE HAY

3. I just cannot get motivated to do anything.

I was going to put this challenge in Part 3 of this book, which focuses on school, until I saw the "to do anything" bit and thought it was better off here. You've probably heard of the carrot-and-stick approach. Carrot-and-stick describes the two ways we can motivate ourselves. The carrot is the reward, and so the carrot method is when you work towards something because there's a reward at the end of it. The stick is the punishment, and so the stick method is when you work towards something because you're trying to avoid the unpleasant consequences of not doing it. Think about it: Are you moving towards things that you want, or moving away from things that you don't want?

Here's an example to help you:

The Carrot Approach: *I'm working hard for this exam because I really want to have a wide range of universities to choose from next year.* (This person is moving towards what they want.)

The Stick Approach: *I'm working hard for this exam because otherwise my parents are really going to be on my case.* (This person is moving away from what they don't want.)

⏸ Which phrase do you find yourself saying more?

There's no right or wrong way, of course; it all depends on your preference and it may vary depending on the situation. One person might run because they want to stay fit, and someone else might run because they don't want to have brittle bones when they're older. Think about the people you know. Why do they do the things they do?

PART 1: PERSONAL • 33

⏸ Think of something you like doing:

Why do you do this thing?

⏩ Think of something you want to achieve:

Now write down why you want to achieve it:

What's important to you about achieving that?

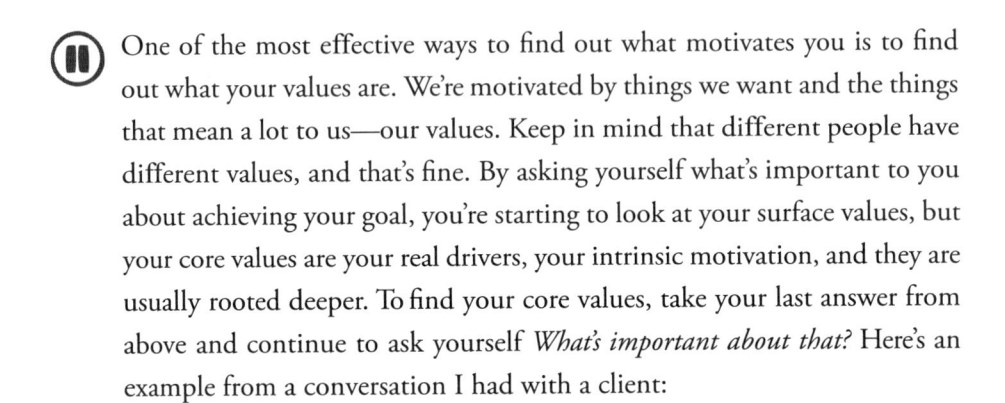

⏸ One of the most effective ways to find out what motivates you is to find out what your values are. We're motivated by things we want and the things that mean a lot to us—our values. Keep in mind that different people have different values, and that's fine. By asking yourself what's important to you about achieving your goal, you're starting to look at your surface values, but your core values are your real drivers, your intrinsic motivation, and they are usually rooted deeper. To find your core values, take your last answer from above and continue to ask yourself *What's important about that?* Here's an example from a conversation I had with a client:

Me: Think of something you want to achieve.
Client: To have my own house by the time I'm twenty-two.
Me: What's important to you about achieving it?
Client: Because I want to have my own space.
Me: What's important to you about having your own space?
Client: So I can have friends around whenever I want.
Me: What's important about having friends around whenever?
Client: Um, it's important because friends are important.

Me: What's important about friends?
Client: They are there for you and they help you.
Me: What's important about someone being there for you and helping you?
Client: It's important to provide support and have support.
Me: What's important about providing and having support?
Client: You need support to achieve. You can't do things on your own; support is key.

BINGO! This person has just told you that they value support tremendously, and it sounds like it is one of their core values. When we started the questions, it sounded like it was all about their own space or being with friends—and of course, those things are important and clearly valuable to this person—but giving and receiving support is one of the bigger, or core, things for them. Ask yourself the same set of questions and write down your response. Often, it's your immediate response that is key, as it comes from your subconscious mind, or your deeper level of mind, so just go with it!

▶ Think of something you want to achieve:

⏸ What's important to you about achieving this?

And what's important about that?

And what's important about that?

And what's important about that?

When you have found what some of your key drivers are, you have an idea of what motivates you, and now you can use it as a key to ignite your own motivation. But how? Well, I will now show you how satisfying your key drivers in any activity you are procrastinating over will motivate you to do it. Let's use the example from above where the key driver was having and giving support. It may turn out that this person who values support—let's call him Dave—likes to do things as part of a team because of the support that team provides. Dave might be shying away from a project because he's worried he has to do it alone and that's not something that's going to motivate him. Once Dave knows that one of his key drivers is support, teamwork, or being around others (remember, it's about what support means to Dave), he can use this and see if someone else will join him in the project, increasing his motivation.

If intrinsic motivation is when we satisfy our core values or something inside of us, then extrinsic motivation is an external factor, maybe materialistic, like a reward or avoiding pain or punishment. If Gillian's need is making money, then she knows if she can find a way to make money out of an activity she undertakes, she is more likely to do it. When Gillian knows that if she doesn't get home by 10 p.m., her parents will ground her, she is more likely to meet their demand and be home by 10 p.m. to avoid being grounded. Both of these examples are extrinsic motivational factors.

Parents use a lot of extrinsic motivation A LOT! As a teacher, I saw it for years in our parent-teacher meetings. "Well, she knows that when she improves her grades, she can go to the concert she wants to go to", which is an example of providing a reward of some kind. "We've made it clear that we'll remove his laptop from him for two weeks if he doesn't study more", which is an example of punishment. I rarely heard "Come on now, son, surely getting higher test scores appeals to your inner desire for fulfilment and achievement." Does this work for everything? Can I use it to get myself out of bed in the morning and not press snooze three times when the alarm goes off? Or to clean my room when I'm being asked to?

Of course you can, you've just got to turn it into something that is of value to you. Something that drives you to achieve it (intrinsic), or come up with some kind of a reward for yourself (extrinsic). Whatever it is, your targets or goals have to be compelling enough for you to be motivated to do it.

⏩ Time to test the theory! Think of something you want to do but you're not really motivated to do it:

What stops you from doing this activity?

What would have to be there for you to be motivated to do this activity? What would you need to have or what would you have to get out of it? Be realistic!

Can you create a link between this activity and something that motivates you intrinsically? Or what kind of extrinsic reason can you come up with for completing this task now?

KEY TAKEAWAYS FROM THIS CHAPTER:

❶

We're motivated by intrinsic factors like our personal desire to do well and extrinsic factors like making money or getting praise. We're also motivated towards things that we want or away from things we don't want.

❷

One way to get yourself motivated is to think about what really matters to you and create a link between that and the task you need to complete.

❸

When you need to stay motivated, remind yourself of all the progress you have made so far and reward yourself for it, too.

"You don't have to be great to start, but you have to start to be great."

— ZIG ZIGLAR

4 Goal setting: How do I even do it?

Setting goals or targets can also really help with motivation. So, while we're on the topic of motivation, let's take a look at goal setting.

▶ In the box below, write down a goal you have.

[ ]

Now I want you to compare these two goals:

| I want to do well in my exams. | I want to get a B in my next French test with Mrs. Trivic in two weeks' time. I want to increase my grammar score by three marks and my comprehension by five marks to get this grade. |

▶ Of the two goals above, which one is better? Which ones shows more focus and is more specific? Which one can be measured more and is more actionable, realistic, and timed? Which one is the SMART goal? SMART is an acronym for goals that are Specific, Measurable, Actionable, Realistic, and Timed. Let's take a closer look to see what it means to have a SMART goal.

- **Specific:** Is your goal focused on something very specific or is it quite vague? What exactly do you want?
- **Measurable/Milestones:** Is there room in your goal to measure your success or how you're getting on with it? You can see in the example above that there is no specific way for us to measure success in the first goal, whereas in the second goal there are figures and milestones to use to measure our progress.
- **Actionable:** What action steps can you take towards your goal? What would those actions look like and when would you plan to carry them out? Our goals won't just magically be achieved; we have to work

towards them, and that means having a set of clear actions to take in that direction. Sure, there are actions we could take towards goal number one, but when we look at goal number two, we can immediately get a clearer picture of what we'd need to do because there's more specific focus on grammar and comprehension.

- **Realistic/Results:** Is it doable? Where are you now regarding achieving that goal? I'm sure both goals are doable, but goal number two makes me think this person has done their homework a little more. They've checked their current mark in French and thought about the areas of the exam where they need to focus on. You can always move the goalposts, just don't move the goal. The "R" can stand for "Results", too. What results will tell you you've achieved this goal? What will they be?
- **Timed:** Your goal has got to have a time frame to it, or it is just a dream. Set yourself mini time frames if it's quite a sizable goal to keep you on track.

Now, using the SMART acronym above, revamp your original goal to make it Specific, Measurable (Milestones), Actionable, Realistic (Results), and Timed.

▶ I want (always start by focusing on what you want):

Once you've set your SMART goal, make sure you tell people about it. Not only does it make you accountable for your goal, but other people can provide support for you, too. Psychologists at Kansas University say that "students with high hopes set themselves higher goals and know how to work hard to attain them".

The next thing I want you to think about is your measures of success or evidence of achieving your goal.

How will you know when you've achieved your goal?

What will you be doing differently?

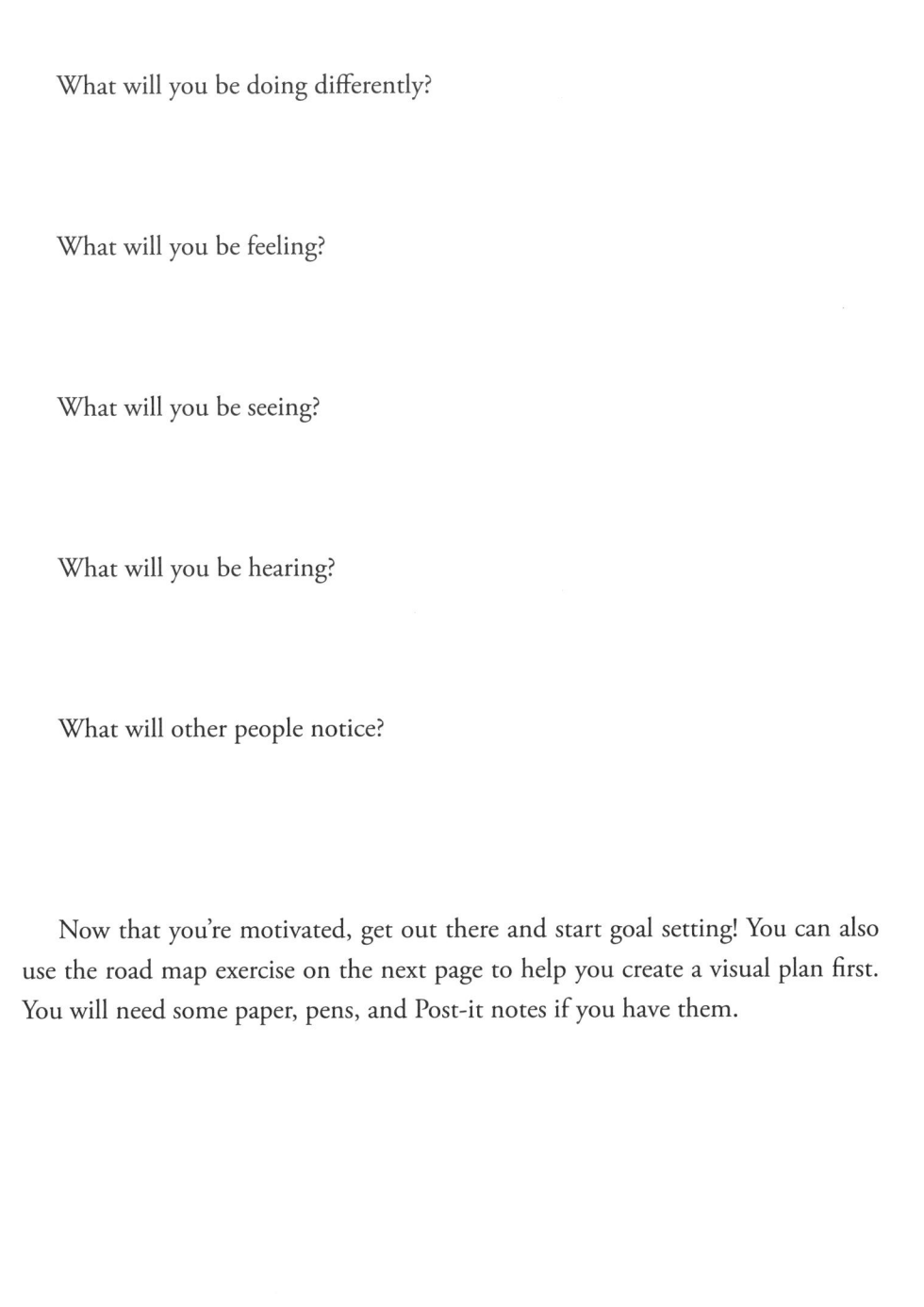

What will you be feeling?

What will you be seeing?

What will you be hearing?

What will other people notice?

Now that you're motivated, get out there and start goal setting! You can also use the road map exercise on the next page to help you create a visual plan first. You will need some paper, pens, and Post-it notes if you have them.

Creating a road map for goal setting

My Goal

Start here with what you have NOW. What resources do you possess?

▶ **STEP 1:** Draw a windy road on a sheet of paper. A3 is probably best so you have plenty of room.

STEP 2: Write out your goal on a Post-it, making sure that it's written in SMART format. If it's not, take time now to revamp your goal and place it at the end of your road.

STEP 3: With any goal, it's important to start with where you are NOW, not where you want to be! So, on another Post-it, write down the resources you currently possess which will enable you to get started on your road. Remember that resources include people who can help, time, constructive thoughts, knowledge, habits, and so on.

STEP 4: Any goal needs milestones along the way. On two more Post-it notes, you're going to identify two milestones you'll need to achieve to measure your success. If your goal is for the end of the year, then make sure you make time to review your progress every sixty to ninety days. Use this time to make any adjustments or amendments.

STEP 5: You need to be realistic when goal setting. Think of any challenges you might have to overcome along the way and mark these in on your road map as a roadblock or detour. This is not being negative; rather, you're being realistic and pragmatic as you will identify ways to overcome these. You cannot predict every single hurdle you may encounter along your way, but you can make sure that you learn to become the most resourceful person you know.

STEP 6: Show how you can overcome the hurdles you've identified. What resources do you have at your disposal? Think of those you identified at the start of your road map. Could it be that you will need more resources? What can you do to obtain these resources?

STEP 7: Is there anything else you need to mark in on your road map? Is there anything that will help you along the way? Are there any major events you need to take into consideration?

STEP 8: Make your goal public! Be accountable for your goal. Put your goal map somewhere where you will see it every day.

KEY TAKEAWAYS FROM THIS CHAPTER:

❶

Goal setting is about getting very clear on what you want, because if you don't know what you want, how will you ever know when you get it?

❷

Write your goals in positive language, starting with "I want", and make sure they are SMART: Specific, Measurable, Actionable, Realistic, and Timed.

❸

Start to visualise what it will be like having achieved this goal—what will you be doing, feeling, hearing, and seeing when you've achieved your goal?

> "A goal without a deadline is just a dream."
>
> — ROBERT HERJAVEC

5 Everything is up in the air for me right now, and I've no idea where to even begin to sort it out.

It's easy to say "just begin at the beginning", isn't it? But we've got to find the beginning, and this is easier said than done. So, in this section, I'm going to introduce you to a Wheel of Life, and we'll go from there. In my coaching experience, I've noticed that people make greater effort to solve the easy problems in their lives and tend to leave the difficult ones in the hope they'll magically solve themselves! But think about how good things would be if you were able to take those things that are up in the air and ground them so you could begin to deal with them one by one.

▶ Below is the Wheel of Life you're going to use. The objective of this wheel is to give you a visual image or representation of how things are going for you in all aspects of your life right now. Forget about things that have happened, resist the urge to worry about what could happen, and focus on each aspect of your life right now.

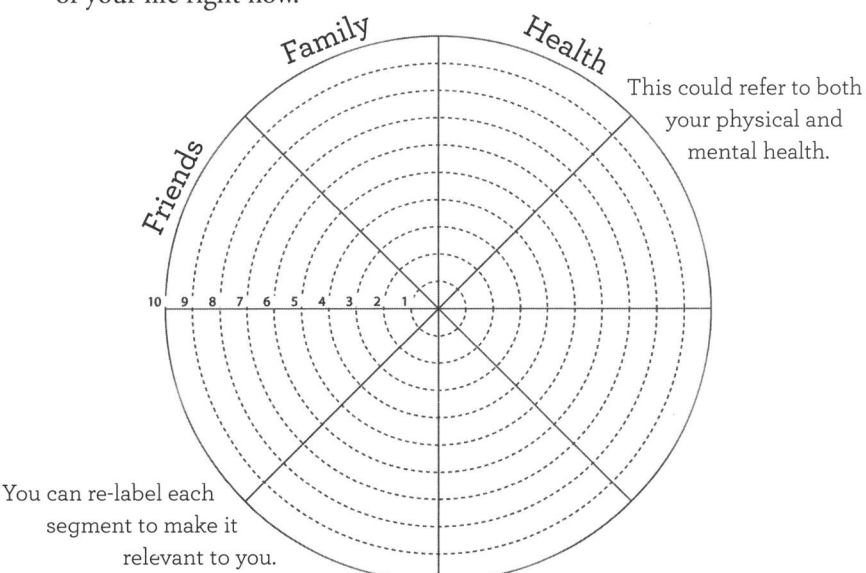

Family — *Health*: This could refer to both your physical and mental health.

Friends

10 9 8 7 6 5 4 3 2 1

You can re-label each segment to make it relevant to you.

PART 1: PERSONAL • 45

1. The first thing I want you to do with your Wheel of Life is to label the segments. Three of them are already labelled, but feel free to label them so that they suit you best. For example: you might label the other segments as School, University Applications, Sport, etc., whatever is important to you right now. You might find that you need to add more segments. Some people divide the Health segment into two; Physical Health and Mental Health as indicated on the wheel.
2. You might find that you need to add more segments.
3. Once you're happy with the labels you've chosen for the segments in your wheel, we're now going to number them to reflect our satisfaction with each one, with 0 being completely unsatisfied and 10 being amazingly satisfied! Here's an example: Imagine I've divided the segment Health into two and I've labelled the two parts Physical and Mental, as we mentioned above. Physically, I might be really healthy, participate in sports, get plenty of sleep, and have a reasonably balanced diet, so I might give myself a 7 in this part of my balance wheel. However, mentally, perhaps there's some things going on in my head that I'm unsure how to deal with. This affects my mood and how I feel about myself, too. A realistic reflection of my mental health might therefore be a 5 on my wheel, as I know I could do more to develop better head space and relax.
4. When you've got a number for each of your segments, and you've marked them in, I want you to connect the lines of the segments together, so you get a better picture of your wheel.

Here's an example:

You can see from the wheel opposite that this person is very happy with their family life. However, it's also clear that there's something going on with this person's friendships at the moment, as they've marked this at 3. Depending on what the rest of this person's wheel is like, they might choose to start working on their friendships to create a more round and balanced wheel.

Now try the following questions.

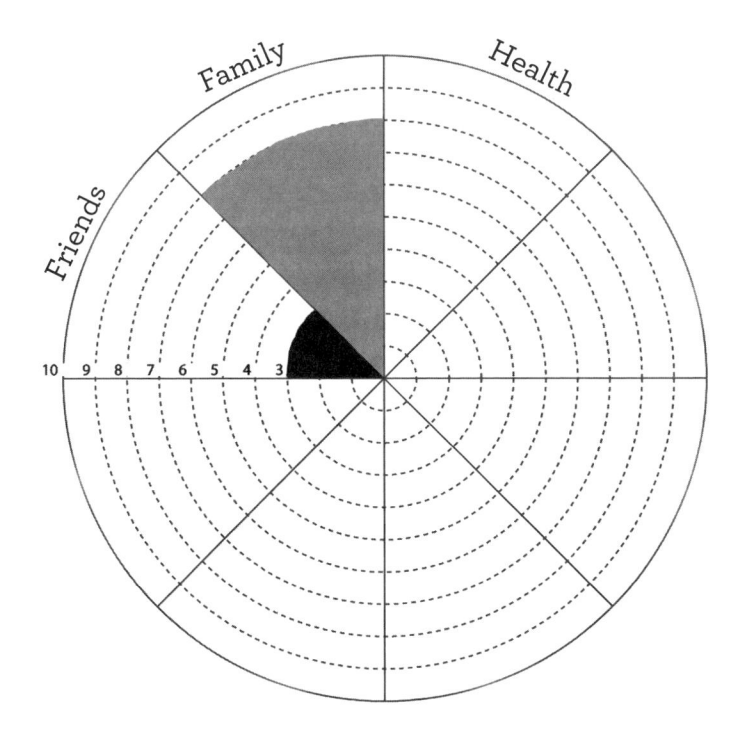

When you look at your Wheel of Life, what do you notice?

Which areas of your life would you benefit from working on? Prioritize them if you can.

What would you gain if you were to work on these areas of your life? You need to make sure it's worthwhile, of course, or you're highly unlikely to make changes!

Can you think of any reasons why you wouldn't want to make these changes? (You've got to make sure it makes sense to your brain to make changes in these areas.)

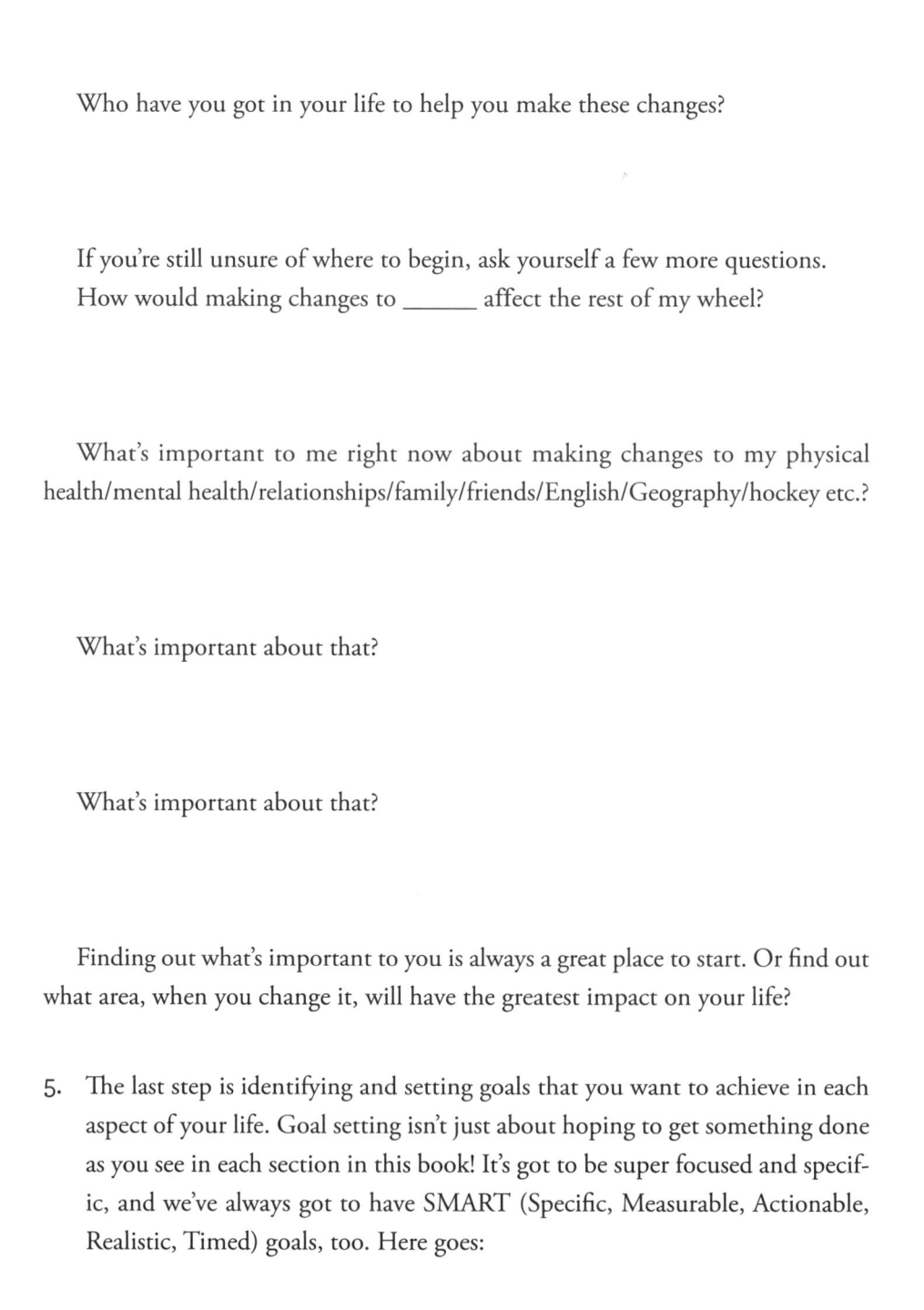

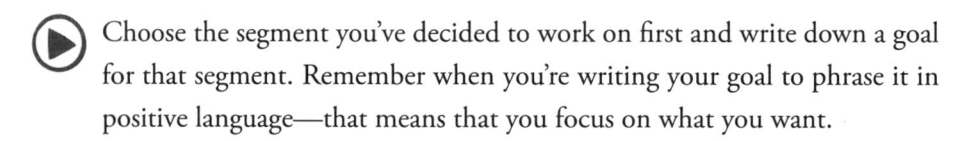

Who have you got in your life to help you make these changes?

If you're still unsure of where to begin, ask yourself a few more questions. How would making changes to _____ affect the rest of my wheel?

What's important to me right now about making changes to my physical health/mental health/relationships/family/friends/English/Geography/hockey etc.?

What's important about that?

What's important about that?

Finding out what's important to you is always a great place to start. Or find out what area, when you change it, will have the greatest impact on your life?

5. The last step is identifying and setting goals that you want to achieve in each aspect of your life. Goal setting isn't just about hoping to get something done as you see in each section in this book! It's got to be super focused and specific, and we've always got to have SMART (Specific, Measurable, Actionable, Realistic, Timed) goals, too. Here goes:

▶ Choose the segment you've decided to work on first and write down a goal for that segment. Remember when you're writing your goal to phrase it in positive language—that means that you focus on what you want.

Goal 1

I want . . .

Recheck your goal for me:

1. Is it specific?
2. Have you identified something very specific to achieve?
3. Is your goal measurable?
4. How will you know when you've achieved it?
5. What will you see?
6. How will you feel?
7. What will you hear from yourself and others?
8. Is your goal achievable? Never change the goal, but sometimes we need to change the goalpost a little.
9. Is this a realistic goal for you to achieve, or do we need to break it down a little more?
10. What's your time frame?

Remember, a goal without a date is just a dream!

Taking the SMART formula into account, I want you to rewrite your goal:

Now we're ready!

Let me share another conversation I had with a client as an example of setting SMART goals here:

Me: Okay, so you were talking about setting yourself a new goal in terms of your fitness. What is it that you want?
Client: I want to be fitter.
Me: Great! What does "fitter" mean to you?
Client: I want to be able to run quicker. I like doing 10K races and I'm getting good at them, so I'd like to be able to run my next 10K in fifty minutes.
Me: Excellent. Is this a realistic goal for you?
Client: Yes, I think so, Linda. I run 10K in fifty-two minutes now, so it's just two minutes. If I put more effort into my training, I can easily do that in four weeks.
Me: Four weeks?
Client: Yup, the next 10K race is in four weeks. It gives me time. I think this is a nice goal.
Me: It sounds like you're starting to create a SMART goal for yourself here. Well done. How will you know when you're on track for this goal?
Client: There's an 8K race with school in ten days, so I can use that to see how I'm getting on.
Me: Sounds good. With this 10K goal, how will you know when you've been successful in achieving it?
Client: When I see that time on my watch, of course!
Me: Fantastic! Well, it sounds like you've got the makings of a strong SMART goal here for yourself. Put this all together for me now and tell me what you want, being as specific as you can.
Client: Sure, so I want to run my next 10K in four weeks in fifty minutes
Me: A bit different from just saying you want to be "fitter", isn't it?
Client: Yes! And I'm more excited about this one, too. By doing this I'll get fitter; that's like the bigger picture.

From this short piece of a conversation, you can see the difference that getting specific can make, as my client went from talking about the bigger picture to talking about what they want to do now. We carried on the conversation to find my client's starting point, resources they have, and resources they need to carry on and achieve their goal.

I talk more about motivation and goal setting in the School section too, where we will also look at creating a road map to success.

KEY TAKEAWAYS FROM THIS CHAPTER:

❶

Use your Wheel of Life to help you gain clarity on what's really going on in your life right now. Remember, it doesn't matter where you are in each segment, it's about what you can do to move forward and create greater balance.

❷

You can create separate wheels for different areas of your life, too, so if school is a big focus at the moment, why not create a specific wheel to gain some clarity in this area, with segments for each of your subjects and your study schedule?

❸

Create mini SMART goals for each segment of your wheel to help you move closer to where you want to be.

"The way to get started is to quit talking and begin doing."

— WALT DISNEY

6 Surely there's a one-stop formula to overcome the challenges I'm facing? Or is that positive thinking?

Positive thinking is great, I'm a huge fan of it. In fact, I'm usually 99.9 percent full of it. And the other tiny percentage? Well, that's when reality has got to come to visit. I can't live my life believing that simply by thinking positively this book will write itself. There's got to be a realistic action that accompanies those optimistic thoughts I possess.

Positive thinking alone won't get you where you want to be. It won't prevent you getting there, but it's even more powerful when accompanied by action. To answer the question above in a nutshell: no, it's not just positive thinking that will help you overcome challenges.

What will help me?

It's all about getting things out of your head so you can work through them logically and rationally. Are you lucky enough to know someone who always knows what to do when a situation arises? I do, quite a few actually, but the two people that spring to my mind immediately are my best friend, Aideen, and my amazing husband, Stephen. Whenever I have raised a problem I've been facing with them, they've mulled it over and said, "Okay, let's look at our options." Aideen in particular will go through a mental Filofax and consider different actions I could take. She'll identify different solutions, and because of her ability to think strategically, she'll also consider a range of consequences that could come about as a result. I continually learn so much from her way of thinking. Stephen, while very similar, will usually remind me of the people or the relationships I've built who could perhaps shed some light on my problem, or he'll ask, "Have you thought about looking at it this way?" What have they both got in common? They are both incredibly resourceful people. They know they don't have all the answers, but they know that by using the resources they have, they can at least find a path to an answer.

If you want to become more successful in overcoming challenges in your life, you must become one of the most resourceful people you know. As an ex-teacher, I used to think that resources were anything I could use for my lessons: images, books, the internet, old notes, handouts, puzzles, glitter glue. Okay, there wasn't much glitter glue used in my history lessons, I'm just making sure you're still with me! But when I started coaching, I discovered that resources are so much more than bits of paper. This is the mindset I need you to get into, too. Your resources obviously include books, exam papers, and so on, but resources also include the people you know, your thoughts, your actions, your attitudes, your behaviours, your feelings, your time, your habits, and your characteristics. Now, if you were to make a list of all these resources you have at your disposal, how equipped would you feel?

The Challenge Wall
The Challenge I'm Currently Facing

STEP 1: Identify the challenge you are currently facing and be as specific as you can.

STEP 2: You are going to use the bricks as "resource" bricks to help you either climb over the wall or to break through the challenge you're facing. Think about all the resources you have available to you right now and start labelling them on the bricks. The following list might help you.

1. **Thoughts:** This is a perfect opportunity to revisit the section on thinking errors and then ask yourself *Am I thinking rationally about this situation? What are more constructive thoughts I can have in this situation?*

2. **Feelings:** What are more constructive feelings you could have about this situation? Could it be an opportunity to grow rather than something that is making you feel scared?

3. **Behaviours:** This is your reaction to something in your environment. It's usually a conscious response, unlike habits, which tend to be subconscious. Ask yourself *Are there aspects of your behaviour you could change?* Or, what behaviours would you have to change to get different results?

4. **Habits:** These are things we do subconsciously, without really thinking about them. Some people don't remember brushing their teeth because they do it habitually, every morning without thinking about it. When you reflect on your habits, what are new habits you could develop that would be beneficial to overcoming this challenge?

5. **Actions:** Think about an action like a step you take. What steps could you take right now to begin to overcome this challenge?

6. **Time:** Are you using your time as effectively as you could be? What would it be like if you could create another two hours in your day? What would have to change for you to have more time?

7. **Characteristics:** Think about some of your characteristics, things that come naturally to you such as being kind, being considerate, thinking strategically. Are there other characteristics you could develop in order to overcome the challenge you are facing? Would it help if you were to be more empathic? More assertive?

8. **People:** Who do you know that can help you? Do you know anyone who has overcome this challenge before? Who could you talk to?

9. **Attitude:** Does your current attitude towards the situation help or hinder you? What would be a more constructive attitude to have?

I know some of you who are reading this would benefit from a practical example of how the Challenge Wall can help you. However, instead of going through the same process again, we will look at another tool, the Help and Hinder Table, because you can then use the suggestions in the Help column of this activity to fill in the Challenge Wall. Throughout the book, you are constantly building up your bank of resources. With the Help and Hinder Table—as well as looking at positive resources that will help you, like in the Challenge Wall—you're also listing things to watch out for, things that could prevent you from being successful.

The challenge I am currently facing: Having time to get everything done!		
Resource	Help	Hinder
Thoughts	What's the most urgent and important task I need to do right now? What do I need to prioritize here? Remember, it's about asking yourself better questions.	Thinking I don't have time and saying this phrase to myself or thinking I have too much to do.
Feelings	Feelings of control and empowerment. Feeling like I am managing my time and I am making progress. Making a schedule would help me feel this way.	Feelings of not being in control. Feeling like things are on top of me, like I have no time or like I have too much to do. Feelings of guilt.
Behaviours	Choosing different behaviours. So when my friends are on group chat, I can tell them I'll chat later and turn off my notifications. Rewarding myself if I stick to a schedule.	Making excuses. Looking at my phone with every beep or not putting it on silent. Not turning the TV off when I work.
Habits	Use alarms to move on to different activities. Get up earlier or change my morning routine. Maybe having set times for social media.	Ignoring the alarm and sleeping in until noon. Losing track of the amount of time I spend on my phone. Checking my phone while doing homework.

	The challenge I am currently facing: Having time to get everything done!	
Actions	Create a timetable this afternoon. Speak to my friends and tell them about my newfound motivation in the hope they'll support me! Create a reward chart to get me motivated.	Not creating a schedule, and not doing anything differently. Inaction; not taking steps towards overcoming the challenge
Time	Setting time aside for specific activities. Recognizing others' time is precious too, so perhaps a better habit is to be ready ten minutes before I have to go anywhere.	Spending time aimlessly on the internet with no purpose at all. Procrastination!
Characteristics	Determination: I will do this, I will achieve it. Resilience: I will keep going. Perseverance: personal strength.	Giving up when it gets tough. Not keeping my promises to myself and others or honoring my commitments.
People	My older sister is great at making and sticking to schedules, so I'll ask her. A friend at school is always on time with coursework and seems to find it easy; I'll ask him if he can give me some tips.	Spending time with friends who aren't interested in achieving goals. Deciding to give up on my goals so I can spend more time hanging out with them.
Attitudes	Developing and maintaining a "growth mindset" where I see any setbacks as opportunities to learn, grow, and do better. Seeing any feedback I get on my work as a chance to learn and improve.	Keeping a "fixed mindset" where I believe everything has to go my way and if it doesn't, I just give up on my project. Taking any feedback very personally and feeling attacked. Refusing to take feedback on board.

Notice that when you think about what feelings might help you cope with this sense of being overwhelmed, your brain might well identify an action you could do in order to start feeling this helpful emotion. We have to do something to get the feeling we want; we have to take action. Filling in the hinder side of the table will help you recognize the habits you have that you need to change in order to complete your tasks on time.

The Challenge Wall and the Help and Hinder Table are two really useful tools to help you deal with challenges. When I use these with clients, the one piece of feedback I always get is that people forget how many resources they actually have available to them. Writing things down highlights just how resourceful our lives actually are.

KEY TAKEAWAYS FROM THIS CHAPTER:

❶

While having a positive attitude and positive thoughts is great, we need to support these with positive action steps to overcome the challenges we're facing.

❷

Step back from the challenge and make a list of all the resources you currently possess to help you overcome the challenge. What characteristics have you got? What knowledge do you have that will help you move past this?

❸

Successful people ask themselves better questions to move forward. Have you ever faced a challenge like this before? If so, how did you deal with it? How would someone you admire deal with this issue?

"Positive thinking is great, but nothing happens without action."

— LINDA BONNAR

7 I worry all the time, about everything.
8 I get anxious about the little things to the point where it makes me feel sick.

I decided to tackle worry and anxiety together because while they may appear similar, there are key differences, and it's important to know them. Let's look at some of them below before we move forward.

1. Worry is thinking about a potential problem in our heads, but anxiety can be felt in your body, too.
2. Anxiety affects how we think, how we feel, and what goes on in our bodies (it might cause our heart to beat faster or give us stomach pains, for example), but worry does not.
3. Worry tends to be mainly made up of words, but anxiety contains both words and mental images—hence it affects our emotions more.
4. Worry tends to be very specific, but anxiety tends to be very general. For example, you could be worried about a test at school but anxious about school in general.
5. We might worry about things that are realistic, like an issue our friend is going through, but get anxious about unrealistic things.
6. Worry doesn't impact your general personal functioning, but anxiety does.

We all worry at some points, it's natural, and in some cases, it can be very helpful, as it reminds us to take particular caution. But when worrying starts to hinder your daily life, it's really time to address triggers or underlying issues.

⏪ The language we use about ourselves is incredibly powerful. *I worry all the time, about everything.* Two words here are immediately ringing alarm bells! These words are "all" and "everything". They're "universals" and often appear under the thinking error of All-or-Nothing Thinking that we saw in

PART 1: PERSONAL • 59

Chapter 2. For example, "There was *nothing good* about my holiday". When that little alarm rings in my head, it is followed by the questions looking for the evidence: *Are you worried ALL of the time? Really?* and *EVERYTHING? Really? Are you worried about reading this sentence right now?* The first step I'd like you to take here is to redefine and be very clear about what you are actually worried about or when these feelings of worry are triggered. See, you weren't born a worrier—none of us were! Worrying is a type of learned behaviour. So, where did we learn it? Where did it all start?

Firstly, when do you not worry? Or what do you not worry about?

What is it about these particular situations that don't cause you to worry?

Now that we've cleared that up and know we don't worry all the time, write down one thing you do worry about:

What is it about this thing that causes you to worry? (We're looking for the trigger to your worry here because when we know the trigger, we can control it.)

If you're having difficulty finding the trigger, use the following to help you: Think about a time when you felt really worried. What was happening? What could you see? What could you hear? Who was there? (I want you to write these down so you can clearly figure out where or what this trigger is. Remember to get it out of your head and onto paper.)

You might find you need to rewind the film you have of the situation in your head so you can really find that trigger. Let's take a common example of this to help you understand. One day I walked into my classroom and said to my class of exam students, "Okay, let's start". Now, to me, that seemed like a fairly harmless statement to make as a teacher walking into her classroom. My intention was to communicate *No chit-chat, you're an exam group. Let's get on with it.* However, my students interpreted my statement completely differently. They stared at me, panicked. I heard them ask one another, "Start what?" and "Have we got a test I don't know about?" One of my students asked, "We're confused! What are we starting?" I explained that I just wanted to start teaching, and they all looked relieved. They thought I was going to give them an exam because apparently, I always say "Let's start" before an exam (Trigger 1). Another student said that I looked very serious when I walked in, like I meant business (Trigger 2).

Of course, my first reaction to all this was *Test face? I have a test face?!* For a few students in my class, they used my facial expressions to detect my mood, and they had learned to become worried when they saw certain expressions on my face. Other students had associated my phrase, "Let's start", with what I say before an exam. A trigger for worry doesn't have to be a huge thing like hearing the ceiling fall; for some people it can be a phrase or a facial gesture. Make time to think about the last time you felt worried, and then we can start to work on a more constructive reaction to it.

Here's another example that maybe many of you will also be familiar with. When I was younger, something that triggered worry in me was hearing our dad shout out our names in a particular voice. That was the trigger for the negative thought cycle which usually consisted of *I wonder if he knows about X?* or *What if he found out about Y?* And then the "what if" train started off. As I got older, I noticed that receiving emails from certain people triggered feelings of worry in me, especially if they didn't use my name in the opening of an email, or if they wrote in a really short and curt way. I would immediately ask myself *What have I done? What if . . . ?* This is very similar to the catastrophizing thinking error we mentioned earlier in Chapter 2.

So, how can you deal with worry? For small-scale things, you can reply to a "what if" question in your head with a *So, what if?* and come up with a rational and logical response to quell your worry.

▶ Answer the following "what if" questions, imagining that your best friend has come to you with these worries.

1. What if I don't meet the deadline for the project?

2. What if I tell that guy/girl I like him/her?

3. What if I ask that question and everyone laughs at me?

⏸ Reread your answers while keeping your thinking errors from Chapter 2 in mind. Let's have a look at some other "what if" questions and some possible answers you can use.

1. *What if they find out I did that thing?* So what if they do? You can handle it. You need to choose a constructive reaction. Is it something you just need to accept? Do you need to apologize for something?
2. *What if she gives us a test and I don't do well?* So what if she does? You cannot control the teacher and the decisions she makes. You can do your best to keep up with your revision as well as you can and use your result to identify areas of the work you need more time with.
3. *What if he/she doesn't reply to the message I sent?* So what if they don't reply? Can you control their reactions? No! Again, realize that you can't control how others react, you can only control your reactions. If they reply, great—and if not, well, that's just how it is.

Sometimes we worry because it's a habit we've picked up from other people in our lives, like our parents or relatives. I have worked with some adults who were constantly worried about money because that's what they heard their parents argue over when they were younger. Unfortunately, many of us take on the worries of our parents, or we want to share them in a bid to help carry the burden. Uncertainty can also be a trigger for worry, as we don't know what the future holds for us or our families. As much as you can plan and prepare for these things, so much is out of our control, and we've simply got to choose the most constructive reaction that we can at the time.

▶ Another thing you can do with thoughts of worry is to check them out, explore them, and see if they are actually a warning sign to do something or take an action step. Is there an action you can take to solve the worry right now? Could you be worrying about something you can do nothing about? Or could you be worrying because it's a habit you've fallen into whenever something like a class test comes up? Remember, if you're unsure whether the worrying thought is helping you to take action and create a solution, or hindering you and holding your back, simply check it out! If in doubt, always probe a little deeper.

⏸ Let's imagine you're worried about an exam.

If your thought is *Worrying about this exam has just helped me to realize I haven't actually opened the book in three weeks because I've been avoiding it, and I know I can do better*, this is a helpful thought!

If your thought is *I've been studying this topic loads, but I still worry before an exam because I still might fail it*, alarm bells need to ring here because this is not helpful. There is no evidence to support this worry about failing the exam. This is the kind of thought that can spiral out of control and begin to cause anxiety.

▶ In coaching, we often use a timeline of our lives to deal with certain issues, and this is a technique you can use to deal with something like worry. If you can, I'd recommend doing this exercise with a friend so that you can say your answers out loud. It helps you get out of your head.

1. Imagine a timeline of your life right in front of you and divide the line into three parts: past, present, and future.
2. Step onto the part of your timeline that represents your present and identify very clearly what it is you are worried about.

3. Now step into a near point in your future, a point when you have solved this issue that was worrying you. You need to see yourself having really successfully dealt with the problem. You can make this more vivid by really visualizing yourself clearly and having your friend ask simple questions such as "What did you have to do to solve that issue?", "What resources did you use?", and "How did you use them?"
4. It's almost like you're making a quick trip to the future to find out how you did something, then you're taking it back to "present you". Some people find it helpful to turn around on the timeline to face the "present you" and actually send them a message of what they need to do.
5. Use the message!

"Worrying is like a rocking chair: It gives you something to do, but never gets you anywhere."

— ERMA BOMBECK

Okay, let's now take a look at anxiety. Like I said at the beginning of this section, we all worry, it's natural, and it often helps us to identify some risks involved in a certain situation to problem solve, which is great. Here's a quick example of this: *I'm worried this book won't sell!* Remember that we can choose how we react to anything. I can choose to see this worry as something restrictive that might stop me pursuing my goal of writing altogether (Hinder). Or I can choose to see it as a little warning sign or a reminder to do more research on publishing houses that cater to young people, or look at other books in the same field and see how well they are doing (Helpful). There's loads I can do, and a first step would be to see how I can use my thoughts constructively.

Now, what happens if this thought is keeping me awake at night? Or if I wake up in floods of sweat because of it? What if I allow this thought to escalate into something bigger, where it begins to affect my work and make me question my ability as a coach? What happens when I can't actually concentrate on other areas of my work because of this problem, or if it begins to affect my relationships? Am I still worried? No, I'm now anxious, and anxiety can be incredibly debilitating.

Be under no illusions at all: anxiety is a serious issue. It is a mental health issue, and if you are concerned you are battling anxiety, you must speak to someone. If the anxiety becomes severe, then you may need to speak to a medical professional. Depending on the severity, it may be recommended that you take medication or receive another form of treatment. The great thing is that there are loads of treatments available nowadays.

Let me tell you a little bit about my experience with anxiety, which will hopefully help you to see that a) you are not alone if you are battling anxiety, and b) you can get through it.

For years when I was younger, I rarely worried, and I definitely didn't get anxious. As a young student, my life consisted of school and going to the equestrian center where I worked and kept my horse—that was it. The other people I competed against never bothered me, the height of the fences, remembering my dressage tests, or even falling off just didn't faze me that much.

Of course, there were times I worried, like if I had a big competition or if I was riding a new horse, but my dad would say it was natural, a sign I was ready to compete, so that's how I saw it. I never recalled being anxious. But sometime when I was about twenty, that all changed and anxiety slowly crept in and took ahold of me. At the time I had no idea what was happening; I didn't have the mind-management skills I do now, and so I had no way of controlling what was going on. I knew it was something worse than worry because of the way it was affecting me (remember, worry is in our heads, but anxiety is in our bodies). By the time I was about twenty-two, my anxiety got so bad that I found I couldn't leave the house on time in the morning to get to work. I used to get myself so worked up that I would be sweating profusely even though I'd just showered, my stomach was constantly in a knot, my mood was so negative, and it was all made worse because I was barely eating. I became anxious about crowds and found myself locked in a public bathroom in a bookstore in Dublin one afternoon, crying because the place was so busy and I felt completely helpless. On another occasion I worked myself up into a frenzy, so much so that I actually passed out in a toilet cubicle in the train station. I felt completely out of control and I was barely keeping it together.

So, what did I do? I knew I needed help and I knew the anxiety wasn't the only thing I needed help with. I don't know if the anxiety was triggered by the eating disorder I had developed or the depression either, but when I did manage to sit down with a doctor and explain everything I was experiencing, he told me that it was quite common for people with eating disorders and/or depression to develop anxiety and vice versa. I remember thinking it sounded like a big knot, like the one that constantly sat in my stomach.

I was prescribed medication to help me deal with the anxiety disorder and the depression, and I started seeing a psychiatrist and nutritionist to help me overcome the eating disorder. I was done with not feeling in control of my life. I was done with all the lies I felt I had to tell for not going to social occasions or for cancelling last minute because I just didn't want to leave the house for whatever reasons, and this time I was ready to make the changes I had to.

While the medication and the talking did help, I knew I needed tools and techniques so that I could gain more control and manage myself better. Because I talk more about the eating disorder and depression in the next section on Friends, I'll share a few things that worked for me in dealing with the anxiety here. Remember that everybody is different and sometimes we have to take some time to try out a few things to find something that will work for us.

1. I started becoming more aware of that little voice of anxiety in my head and challenging it rather than letting it take control.

2. While I didn't ride at the time and I hadn't discovered my love for running, I loved getting out walking and always felt so much more relaxed afterwards.

When I knew I had to face a crowd in a shop or a busy train station, I would take deep breaths and repeat my little mantra of *You've got this* in my head (I still use this today but I've "upgraded" it with the image of me walking somewhere really peaceful with all the time in the world, and it works like a treat!).

▶ What can you do?

1. Firstly, if you are worried about yourself personally or about a friend, please speak to someone.
2. Become more aware of the thoughts that you allow to take center stage in your head and use the chart from Chapter 2 on thinking errors to replace them with more constructive thoughts.
3. Learn to relax more with a form of mindfulness meditation like Headspace, which is a fun app you can use on your phone. Or you could read one of the many mindfulness books that are available to see how you can learn to focus on the present more.
4. Deep breathing isn't just for yogis or hippies! If you learn to control your breathing, you'll also learn how to slow down your thought processes too. Inhale slowly through your nose for a count of five, hold the breath for five seconds, and then exhale slowly through your mouth for a count of five. Do this ten times and notice the change.
5. Do your best to get out and about and get your body moving. Exercise is phenomenal for reducing worry, stress, and anxiety in your life. I once read in a copy of *Runner's World* that the whole act of moving forward gets your brain to think forward and actually work to solve some of the issues you're worried about. Remember, you don't have to be a runner for this to work—get out and walk, jog, cycle, swim, whatever!

KEY TAKEAWAYS FROM THIS CHAPTER:

❶

While worry and anxiety appear similar, they are very different. We tend to worry about specific things like getting along with a specific person in our class but feel anxious about meeting new people in general. It's natural to worry about some things, but anxiety can stop us functioning properly.

❷

Worries and anxieties live in the future. By practicing being focused on the present (mindfulness), we can learn to quiet these kinds of thoughts and control them better.

❸

Deep breathing and repeating a strong empowering mantra to yourself is something you can do anywhere at any time to calm yourself down. Remember to breathe in for a count of five, hold the breath for a count of five, and slowly exhale for a count of five.

"Life is 10 percent what happens to me and 90 percent how I react to it."

— JOHN C. MAXWELL

9 I'm totally stressing about life in general.

What is stress and what does it mean to be "stressed"?

Stress is a normal physical response to events that make you feel threatened or that upset your balance in some way. We need a certain amount of stress in our lives to a degree. When working properly, stress helps us stay focused, energetic, and alert, like when we're working to meet an important deadline. We tend to say that we feel stressed when we feel overloaded; life has placed too many demands on us and we are worried that we won't be able to cope. In the "flight or fight" response, stress kicks in and tells you to run from that ferocious lion chasing you. However, unlike our caveman ancestors, we don't face predators like lions anymore, so beyond a certain point, stress stops being helpful and starts causing major damage to your health, mood, productivity, relationships, and your quality of life. And anything that reduces your quality of life is a huge no-no for me!

It's important to mention that stress is also different from anxiety because while we see that a little bit of stress can help us be productive and get things done, like meeting that deadline, this is not the same with anxiety. Stress is usually short-term and tends to vanish when the situation is dealt with, like an exam, but anxiety is different because it lingers on and doesn't go away even though you've dealt with the "threat" or the "stressor."

How do I recognize stress? Here's a list of the main symptoms.

Cognitive	Emotional
Memory problems	Moodiness or short-temper
Inability to concentrate	Agitation
Poor judgment	Feeling overwhelmed
Seeing only the negative	Sense of loneliness or isolation
Worrying or racing thoughts	Depression

Physical	Behavioural
Aches, pains	Eating more or less than usual
Constipation	Sleeping more or less than usual
Nausea	Isolating yourself from others
Dizziness	Procrastinating responsibilities
Chest pains	Nervous habits (nail biting, pacing)
	Using substances to relax

Please remember that eating more or less than usual once in a while does not necessarily mean you are stressed, and neither does fancying a night in to yourself rather than seeing friends. But when a combination of these symptoms are frequently and consistently present over a period of two weeks, it could be a sign that you are stressed. Keep in mind that I am not a medical doctor, and while these could be indicators of stress, they could also be indicators or other medical issues, and as always, if in doubt, see your local GP.

▶ What can you do?

A lot of stress management comes down to self-management, and that's not always easy, I know. But if you can learn to manage certain stressors (a source of stress) in your life at this early stage, or manage your reaction to certain situations in your life, by the time you get to my age you'll be taking life's events all in stride. I'm going to give you a few quick fixes you can use if you find yourself feeling stressed, and then we'll look at some long-term changes you can implement. Okay, quick fixes first. You might find that some of these overlap from the previous chapters, but it just means they'll be reinforced in your brain more.

1. Fix your posture and fake it until you make it! Fake being relaxed and in control. This is often referred to as the "as if" method. So, you act "as if" you feel differently, just like how I mentioned in the Superman/Superwoman Pose. It's not about ignoring the issue that's present, but it's about getting yourself into a confident state that will allow you to remember to lean on the resources you identified when working on the Challenge Wall. Take a deep breath, push

your shoulders back, hold your head up high, and tell yourself *I can do this, I'll find a way.*
2. Laugh! "Laughter is the best medicine". Obviously not appropriate in every situation, like in an exam hall, but you get the picture. According to helpguide.org, "Laughter is a powerful antidote to stress, pain, and conflict. Nothing works faster or more dependably to bring your mind and body back into balance than a good laugh. Humor lightens your burdens, inspires hopes, connects you to others, and keeps you grounded, focused, and alert". I rest my case.
3. Remove yourself from the situation. Get out for a quick walk or breath of fresh air to help you see the situation differently.
4. Deep breathing. Slow down your breathing, slow down your thoughts, and you'll gain control. We mentioned this in the section on worry and anxiety, so here's a good time to introduce you to Elevator Breathing. You've nothing to lose by giving this a go, and it is particularly helpful for those of you who are highly visual.

Elevator Breathing

STEP 1: Imagine you're on the ground floor of a really tall building, from which you'll be able to see an incredible view when you reach the top.

STEP 2: Invite some of your family and friends into the elevator with you so they can enjoy the view from the top, too.

STEP 3: Now you're going to control how quickly the elevator rises with your breath. You want your family and friends to have a smooth ride to the top, so when you're ready to, inhale deeply while counting to five, allowing your elevator to climb higher. Once you've practiced this for the count of five a few times, you can challenge yourself to inhale for longer.

STEP 4: You're going to hold the elevator at the top for everyone to enjoy the view by holding your breath. Once you've inhaled for a count of five, now I want you to hold your breath and count to five. Remember the longer you hold your breath, the longer everyone gets to enjoy the spectacular view!

STEP 5: Again, using your breath you're going to control how the elevator travels back to the ground, nice and gently, by exhaling slowly for a count of five. Once you're done, open the doors of the elevator and thank everyone for coming on the ride with you! Great work!

5. Write down how you are feeling. Admit it to yourself. Writing things down can be very cathartic. And as I've said before, it's great to get things out of your head and onto paper where you have a greater chance of dealing with things in a logical and rational manner.

6. Gain greater perspective. In coaching, this is often referred to as the Helicopter Position, and if it's helpful, you can actually visualize yourself getting into a helicopter and flying above the situation to see it from different angles. Taking a new position to view the situation can be really helpful, as it can help your relationship with the other people involved as you learn to see things from their perspective. Imagine the helicopter takes off, and you fly high above the situation so you can look down on it. What are the other people in the situation experiencing?

Is this similar or different to your experience? How?

What do you know now about the situation having now taken a different perspective on it?

You can use the Helicopter View to ask yourself better questions, too. As you look at the event in question from the helicopter, you can ask yourself *How important is this situation to the rest of my life?*

Is this situation going to last forever or will it pass and things will change?

What are the really important things in your life? Is this one of them, or has it changed them?

7. Develop the habit of asking better questions. Instead of asking *Why is this happening to me?* you can ask better questions that help your brain move towards finding solutions: *What can I do now?* or *What can I do to move forward from this situation?*
8. Download some mindfulness apps onto your phone/iPod and take a short break to help you gather some perspective on the situation.
9. Make a short Happy List that you have access to all the time. Add songs, photos, memories, or video clips to the list. I am one of those people who have go-to photos or YouTube clips that I know are guaranteed to make me laugh or just relax when I need them.

Long-Term Solutions

If you find yourself saying "I feel stressed" quite frequently and not just around exam times or before an important deadline, then it sounds like it's time to change some behaviours and develop more constructive habits. The key takeaway is to learn to control the controllable. You know how much I love constructing and completing a good table, so here we go!

Task 1: The 4As of Stress Management

▶ The 4As of Stress Management (Adapt, Avoid, Alter, Accept) is a great tool to use when you're feeling stressed. Not only does it encourage us to get our thoughts out of our head and onto paper, but it helps us create solutions, too. First of all, write down the problem that's causing you stress at the moment. I'll do an example below for you:

I'm stressed about my final exams in a few weeks.

▶ Now complete the 4As table below using the questions, suggestions, and examples I have given you as a guide.

Adapt I'm going to stop complaining about the exams because that gets me nowhere and develop a more positive attitude about them.	**Avoid** I can avoid spending as much time with people like John who keep talking about how bad the exams are going to be because that's not helping me.
Alter I'm going to be honest with my History teacher and tell him I don't understand the essay structure, which will definitely help me more.	**Accept** Doing exams is a part of the process of me wanting to become a vet, and stressing about them doesn't help.

To answer each of the sections, let's go through a set of questions.

1. **Adapt:** This first part focuses on YOU. If you can't change the stressor, change yourself. Ask yourself *Is there anything I can do to adapt/change to fit the situation at hand? How can I adapt my behaviour, thoughts, actions, words, or reactions to deal with the stressor better?*
2. **Avoid:** There are often plenty of things we can do to avoid stress in our lives. Granted, this isn't always easy, especially if you feel it's a family member involved! Ask yourself *Is there someone in particular I could spend less time with during this period? Is there anything I can say no to at the moment to reduce the stress I'm feeling?*
3. **Alter:** When we can't control all aspects of the stressor (like the example above of exams), we can do our best to create change by communicating openly and honestly and altering how we go about our day. Ask yourself *Who can I speak openly and honestly with about the stressor? How can I create more balance in my day?* Remember that this is not about changing other people, because we can't do this!
4. **Accept:** Some stressful situations are unavoidable, and these are the ones we need to work on accepting because we cannot change them. Ask yourself *Are there aspects of this situation/event that I simply have to learn to accept? What are*

the aspects of the situation that I cannot control? What can I control about the situation?

Here are some other long-term solutions for stress:

1. Find what works for you. Events can often cause us stress, and the best way to deal with something like this is to have a plan of action ready. Practice the different forms of stress relief that we are discussing and see which ones work best for you at various times of stress. Check that you are approaching the situation in the best way with realistic expectations. To do so, take this opportunity to revisit the thinking errors we covered earlier in the book. You can move on from the event by asking yourself better questions and looking at the lessons to be learned from the event, too. An example of something we often need to accept is that some people simply don't think the same way we do. They don't prioritize things that we do, and that's just life. This is where the Helicopter View can become a useful habit to get into. How are the other people involved experiencing the event? Have you had a conversation with them about it? Have you asked what their perspective is?
2. If you stop one thing in life, stop worrying! Sitting around ruminating about something doesn't change it. Instead, it can make the problem seem bigger and bigger—increasingly insurmountable. Remember the resources you have (see Challenge Wall in Chapter 6), and re-read the previous chapter on worry.
3. Change the language you use with yourself and others. Remind yourself of the thinking errors table. Words like "should" and "must" only serve to bring about feelings of guilt, and they often don't work to motivate us. Think about words you can use instead of these, like replacing "should" with "could", for example. How do the following sentences make you feel?

"I should be there to help the team whenever they need it" OR "I could make more time to speak to the team after our training sessions".

"I have to go to training twice a week" OR "I will go to training twice a week".

The sentence with "could" makes it sound like the person has had a choice to make changes in their behaviour, whereas the "should" implies very little choice. Furthermore, it's also highly unrealistic to think you can be there for someone whenever they need it. It creates pressure and guilt, which are rarely helpful! It is the same with the second set of sentences. The first gives me the impression there is no choice, whereas the word "will" in the second sentence makes it feel much more empowering. We often get plenty of reminders about being careful with the words we use with others, but what about reflecting more on the words we use with ourselves?

> What other words or phrases do you frequently use that aren't helpful to your state?

Start to pay attention to the words people around you use, too. How do they talk to themselves? Are they bringing about feelings of guilt and pressure or choice and empowerment?

4. Prevention is better than cure. Like the quick fix idea of "faking it", work on developing a mantra that reminds you of how resourceful you are when something stressful pops up. Your aim here is to prevent a "what if" thought from turning into a full-on stressful situation. A mantra like *I have all the resources I need to deal effectively with this* is great. This type of sentence sends a very different message to your brain, one of resourcefulness, efficiency, calm, and strategic thinking. It is much more constructive than saying *I've no idea what I'm going to do*. Ideally, repeating this positive mantra will become more than just a quick fix; it will become a habit—one of the many resources you have at your disposal. Make sure you say the sentence with the body language to support it: head up, shoulders back, and nod and smile in agreement as you say your phrase.

5. Have realistic expectations of yourself. Sometimes we have unrealistic expectations of ourselves, of others, and of situations, and we find ourselves getting stressed when those expectations are not met. Be realistic about the time you have, of other people's time, and of the number of things you can say yes to, because sometimes we take on too much and don't handle it very well. Accept

that it's realistic and responsible for you to manage yourself, but it's completely unrealistic for you to be responsible for anyone else.

6. Time management. How we use our time is based on how we manage ourselves. Do you need to manage yourself better? Do you need to set more realistic boundaries or expectations as we mentioned above? One of the most used phrases I hear is "I don't have time". And my usual response is "Well, now you need to decide how you're going to make the time". If it's something we really want to do, then we make time for it, and if not, we make excuses. My friend wanted to run a marathon, and she became very dedicated, training like a trooper. As luck would have it, she was offered a wonderful promotion to her dream job at the same time. Amazing. For the first few weeks, her new role became quite demanding of her time, and so, being an effective self-manager, she got up even earlier in the mornings to train. After two weeks of 4:00 a.m. starts and finishing work late in the evenings, she was exhausted and knew something had to give. She made the tough decision to push her marathon goal back a year until she had experience in her new role. She would still run when she had time, but she felt that she needed to say no to the marathon at that time of year to give her dream job more of her attention. Decide if the activities you're undertaking are things you really want to do right now, and if not, then be honest with yourself about it.

7. Prevention is better than cure. Stress is becoming a huge problem and is responsible for about one in three absences at work. Now, while I know you guys aren't heading off to offices in the morning, by learning to manage stressful situations in your life now, you won't be part of these statistics, and you can just take days off for fun instead! I strongly recommend you work on dealing with the little problems as they pop up, because if you sweep them under the carpet, they eventually grow to become bigger things. Your brain often stores things away when it knows you're not in the right place to deal with them, but it WILL bring them back up when it feels you are ready. For example, one day after my coaching course, I was out running when suddenly this incident from my past popped into my head. It completely shocked me because I hadn't thought about it in years and I know why—because at the time it made me feel guilty. I clearly hadn't dealt with it and just swept it under the carpet. But because we had just done an exercise on the course dealing with guilt, my brain now thought it was a good idea to bring this incident up, knowing I was

PART 1: PERSONAL • 77

now in a position to deal with it properly once and for all. Deal with things as they happen as much as possible.

8. Develop a calmer morning routine. How many of you find yourselves rushing around the house in the morning? Or maybe you're the calm one in a house full of others rushing around? Years ago, I began to notice that my first thoughts in the morning were not very positive at all. I would complain as I walked through the apartment, and I would find a whole range of things to moan about, allowing that negative thought cycle to just do its own thing. I had no idea that's how I was setting myself up for the day. Yikes! Let me show you how different things are now.

	Then	**Now**
First words	Aw, man! Work again.	Thank you, thank you, thank you.
First thoughts	MAN! I've not marked my year 12 paper/I've got a meeting this morning/I have to do my long run later.	What am I going to achieve today? How am I going to achieve it? Plus, I now focus more on appreciation.
First actions	Boil kettle for coffee, complain en route to the kitchen!	Drink water, stretch, do my Top Three Things and lessons learned, make a to-do list, begin an activity on my to-do list, make my bed.

Now I don't spend thirty minutes walking around the apartment creating a gratitude list and jumping around like I've won the lottery! Most of the actions above happen in the first ten minutes of me getting up. Sometimes that to-do list is in my head until I sit down to do my Top Three Things, where I make a short gratitude list of just three non-material things. It's a fantastic way to start your morning. If things didn't go my way the day before, then I also use this time to identify lessons I can learn from yesterday. It's a great way to deal with the event, and it also means I don't carry any of the negativity from yesterday into my new day.

▶ What changes could you make to your morning routine? And is there anything you'd have to do to ensure this new routine goes to plan? For example, would it be helpful to place some sticky notes around your room or work area as a reminder? Action steps, people, it's all about action steps! What action steps can you take?

	Then	Now
First thoughts		
First words		
First actions		

I'm not going to tell you that if you follow all of the above suggestions, you will never be stressed again, because that would be a lie! Remember stress is natural and useful in some situations. But there are some things you can do and a number of habits you can begin to develop to prevent stress from becoming a part of your daily life. The key to success here is creating habits. These are new skills, and as with any new skill, you need to practice it regularly to enhance it.

KEY TAKEAWAYS FROM THIS CHAPTER:

❶

While it's natural to feel stressed at some points in our lives, to manage stress better we need to identify the source of it and remember that stress management is not one size fits all; different forms of stress management will work for different people.

❷

If you feel stressed, make a quick mental or written list of the things you can control about the situation and the things you cannot. Then tear up the list of the things you cannot control!

❸

Having a never-ending to-do list can be a cause of stress for many people. Help yourself by distinguishing and prioritizing between tasks that are both urgent and important and tasks you feel you "should" do.

"It's not the load that breaks you down, it's the way you carry it."

— LOU HOLTZ

10 I go on social media a lot, but I notice that it only seems to make me feel worse about myself.

Stop comparing your behind-the-scenes with everyone else's highlight reel! Yes, the "highlight reel" of social media. The millions and millions of profiles that are accessible literally at the touch of our fingertips. There are the Instagram pictures, the Facebook updates, the Snapchat posts, and the tweets that remind us of how they always seem to be having a great time with loads of friends. Then there are the posts of the perfect new clothes they've just bought, the perfect test scores, the perfect sporting performance, the perfect couple that can't get enough of each other . . . All perfect, perfect, perfect!

Let's be honest, social media is just a snapshot of the best bits of someone's life, it's not the full motion picture of real-life events. And yes, I'm guilty of only showing the highlight reel, too. You won't find pictures of me on my wedding day as Aideen, my bridesmaid, desperately tried to zip my dress up, or pictures of me as I hobbled out of a race one day because I needed the toilet so badly, or pictures of me as I wake up first thing in the morning either—no way! You will find the wedding pictures where I'm actually in the dress, the pictures of me post-race with my medal in hand, and me when I've got makeup on! Why? Simply because I don't want people I don't know, who don't know me, seeing me like this on social media. The people who have actually seen me hobble out of races or seen me without makeup at all are already my friends. But for the world to be able to judge me via social media? No thanks!

Here's the point, if you're feeling in any way bad about yourself for whatever reason, then going through your various social media feeds is probably the worst thing you can do because you end up comparing your reality, your behind-the-scenes, with other people's highlight reel. That's not fair on you. So, use this as motivation to do something different, to develop a different routine to make yourself feel better. Break the social media habit. Our habits are formed by a particular cue, followed by a routine, followed by a reward of some kind. It's very logical when we think about it in this way. Now this person is hoping that by going onto social media (routine) when they're feeling down (cue), they'll end up feeling better (reward) about themselves. But this doesn't actually happen, and instead, the person ends up feeling worse about themselves. Hence, to get a different result, you need to change the routine itself. If you want the reward of feeling better about yourself, change the routine. So, what could you do to make yourself feel better instead of going on social media? What would be a more constructive action?

What action would you have to take to change this habit of aimlessly scrolling through social media?

Social media can be a fantastic tool. I love it myself, as it allows me to promote my work and my products, and it allows my business to grow. But if you're not even sure why you do it anymore, then you've already started to question what purpose it serves. How much time do you spend on social media each day? Studies are suggesting that on average, we spend one hour and forty minutes on social media each day. Which of your dreams could you have fulfilled by dedicating almost two hours to it each day?

Your Values and Belief System

You might not know what you would rather spend that one hour and forty minutes a day doing. It's probably not going to always want to be schoolwork or doing chores, and I don't blame you! How about using some of that time to follow your dreams? The following exercise will help you discover your values and belief system, and this in turn will allow you to work out what your dreams are and what you want to work towards. For this exercise, I want you to think of values and beliefs as things you carry around with you every day. It might be helpful to think of them as something you wear all the time. We often refer to our values and beliefs to help guide us through particular situations. For example, if you believe that it is wrong to steal things, then that usually keeps you from doing it! Likewise, if we value honesty in ourselves and others, that encourages us to tell the truth. Identifying and understanding our values and beliefs can also be very helpful in understanding why we are drawn to some people more than others, as we tend to trust those who share our values and beliefs. They can also help us to pinpoint reasons why we might get angry or frustrated with others who don't share our beliefs or don't respect our values. An important point to remember here is that when it comes to values and beliefs, it is NOT a one-size-fits-all kind of thing. Using the analogy of our values and beliefs as an item of clothing, it's not going to fit or suit everyone who attempts to wear it. Have you ever tried your very, very best to convince someone that what you believe is correct, but no matter how hard you try, it's just not working? That's why! Do you ever get annoyed when someone seems not to care about doing something that you would never think about doing? That's why. They just don't share the same values and beliefs as you do.

What's the difference? Simply put, values can be seen as a set of ideas that guide us or help us see the difference between right and wrong. Beliefs are like a set of statements that people hold to be true because of a particular experience. In essence, they believe they have evidence for it. In his book, *The Chimp Paradox*, Professor Steve Peters refers to these as "Truths of Life" and "Values". He differentiates between them beautifully by saying, "The difference between 'Truths' and 'Values' is that 'Truths' are evidence-based, whereas 'Values' are personal judgment calls". Below is an example, and for now, just accept these as someone's values and beliefs without any judgment at all, and we can discuss them later.

Values (judgment calls):
It's better to put other people first./Work always comes first.
Beliefs (the person has evidence of some kind for this):
Good things happen to good people./There's good and bad in everyone.

Considering the values and beliefs this person has (remember—don't judge!), how helpful do you think these are for that person? Taking the values first, if this person puts other people first all the time, what's going to happen? What effect will that have on them? And if they always put work first, then what happens?

If we look at this person's belief system that "good things happen to good people", how much proof do they have for that? How are they defining "good"? Is this a helpful belief? Because surely there are good people who have had bad things happen to them. Further, if they believe there's good and bad in everyone, and this is one of their strongest beliefs, it's great that they will look for the good in everyone, brilliant, but will they then also look for the bad? I'm not saying it's not right to say there's good and bad in everyone; I'm just encouraging you to think about how helpful this system is.

▶ Now identify a set of three values and beliefs you have at the moment and write down how those values and beliefs help you.

Values:	How these helped me:

Beliefs:	How these helped me:

The idea behind doing this is to test your value and belief system to see if what you are carrying around with you every day is helpful, because if it's not, then you need to make changes. If you find your system isn't helpful, then make it helpful. It might take you a few days, it doesn't matter, but do it!

A client once said to me, "But Linda, I'm a good person so good things should happen for me". Now it's lovely that this person feels they are a good person, and because I know them, I can say that, yes, they are. However, as soon as I heard the word "should" in there, the alarm bells started ringing because we know from earlier chapters that the word "should" brings with it guilt and frustration. So, if you're going to use that word with yourself, then just open the door now and invite in guilt and frustration. This was one belief this person held about themselves, and they had gathered evidence to support it. However, when something didn't go the way they expected it to, it led them to question their belief system. They became very frustrated and guilty about the actions they had chosen. Was it a helpful belief? No. By working together, we came up with a more effective belief system, and after a few days this person sent me back their reviewed set of values and beliefs, which I loved. They've agreed it's okay for me to share one or two of them with you—in fact, they were happy I asked them!

New Beliefs:
Bad things happen, even to good people./I can handle change.

What's your immediate reaction to these? When you compare them to the other set of beliefs, what do you notice? Are they more helpful and constructive? Some people might say the first one is negative, but I find it empowering and accepting. They are accepting of the fact that things don't always go their way and that's life. A person who believes this to be true is in a much stronger position to handle such situations as they won't take the event personally or sit around and ask themselves *Why me?* They are therefore more likely to find solutions quicker, too. This person's other belief of being able to handle change is very empowering, especially considering they once held the judgment that change was bad.

New Values:
Putting myself first is being responsible, not selfish./My family comes before work.

You can see huge changes here with this person in what they value in life and what's important to them. They saw that by putting others first all the time, they were left feeling annoyed and like they weren't being true to themselves. In reviewing their values, this person placed family before work because they recognized how much more important these relationships were. It doesn't mean they stopped putting effort into their work; it just means they've changed their priorities. This particular person now uses these values and beliefs to guide them, and things are working out better for them because they've developed a system that's helpful and constructive. This is what I want for you.

Where do our beliefs and values come from? We've been picking up beliefs and values since we were able to! Think of all the people you've spent time with and developed relationships with since you were little, and there you go! Your parents will obviously play a key role in the belief and value system you take with you as you grow. And so, my intent in this chapter isn't to encourage you to doubt your parents or question them—no, my intent is to encourage you to evaluate your own beliefs and values. Essentially it is your beliefs that will limit you or your beliefs that will empower you to achieve amazing things, so choose them wisely.

I grew up seeing, hearing, and feeling that doing things for other people is important and that doing things for yourself first is quite selfish. This belief meant that for years I put other people before myself, which, yes, is a nice thing to do, until one day I thought, you know what, if I do this thing for this person now, then I'm not going to have time to complete my own work, which is important to me. I found myself wondering, when is it okay to say no? When is it okay to put me first? Is it ever okay to put me first? Yes, sometimes, because I've learned that I have a responsibility to myself. Of course, I have a responsibility to help family and friends and those less fortunate than myself, but to do that, I need to help myself first. And so, one of my most recent values is: I have a responsibility to myself to be the best version of myself that I can be.

KEY TAKEAWAYS FROM THIS CHAPTER:

❶

Social media is a great tool for keeping in touch with people, but too much scrolling can have a negative impact on our mental health, as we're more likely to negatively compare ourselves to those we see on our screens. Keep in mind that everyone you see has a behind-the-scenes/screen life too.

❷

If you're trying to spend less time on social media, the next time you find yourself scrolling, ask yourself what your purpose in scrolling is and what's important about it.

❸

Your beliefs and values can become outdated, so just like you update software on a device, make time to update your beliefs and values, too. What do you believe to be true and what are some things that are important to you?

"If you want to feel better about yourself, don't scroll through your social media. Scroll through your skills, your successes, and your strengths instead."

— LINDA BONNAR

Friends

The Challenges Dealt With in PART 2

11. I don't have many friends/I would like more friends.
12. I don't like going to parties, but then I feel left out when it's all my friends talk about.
13. Compared to my friends, I feel fat and unattractive. I've started dieting but can't seem to stop.
14. I feel my friends don't care about me anymore.
15. I'm concerned that my friend might be depressed, and I don't know what to do.
16. My friend is in a toxic and abusive relationship.
17. I'm not sure if I'm jealous or envious of my friends, but either way, it's not a nice feeling. How can I stop it?
18. My friends think I'm really shy, when in fact I'm terrified I'll say the wrong thing to someone I've just met.

continued . . .

19. I feel pressured to do things in my friendship group that I'm just not comfortable with.

20. My friends have started to comment on my temper. I just can't seem to control it. I think I've got anger management issues.

11 I feel like I don't have many friends/I would like more friends.

Firstly, just because we feel this way, doesn't mean it's actually the case. This might sound harsh, but as I'm sure you've noticed already, I'm all about thinking rationally and logically, so let's take a closer look at this.

▶ What would having more friends do for you?

What are three things you could start doing to increase your chances of meeting new people and making new friends?

1.

2.

3.

We like people who are like ourselves, and we like people we have something in common with. In the same way, we tend to stay away from, or even avoid, people who might not share the same values or beliefs as us. Even very early on in childhood, we are good at recognizing children we don't want to play with because of something they said, did, or a certain trait or characteristic they possess. Think about it: it makes sense, right? I mean, who wants to play with the playground bully? Not many kids. But who wants to play with the kids who are willing to share toys? Loads!

▶ Starting point

Find people you have things in common with, and remember this might take time, so don't rush it. But how will you know what people are interested in? Ask them, of course! Think of one person right now that you would like to get to know better:

What's that person interested in?

What's one question you could ask that person to start a conversation with them the next time you see them?

Remember that making friends isn't always as easy as people make out to be, especially if you're not very comfortable in social situations. Sometimes people already have a sports team in common, or a dance class, or a language, but if you've just moved to a new school or you have a different set of hobbies and interests, then it could be a little more challenging. I also want to gently remind you that the best friends you make may not even be within your school community.

When I was younger, all I wanted to do was ride horses. I wanted to be at my local yard all day long. Now, yes, that cliché of young girls loving ponies exists, but actually there weren't that many girls like that at my school. I ended up having stronger friendships with people outside of school who were also into horses. And that's fine—your friends don't have to be at school with you.

What I don't want you to do is to change yourself completely and fake a variety of interests in the hope that this will make you more attractive to people. Integrity is one of the most attractive qualities a person can possess, and this means being honest with yourself. I remember getting interested in football and certain TV programs, all in the hope of strengthening friendships. The funny thing is, this behaviour usually continues as you try to attract a boyfriend/girlfriend, and you pretend to like particular music, movies, and so on. I once pretended to be really into certain bands to impress this guy I fancied—I bought all the albums to listen to, and learnt the lyrics, even though I absolutely hated them! Thankfully the relationship didn't last too long. There were times when new relationships introduced me to different types of music, which I grew to like or appreciate, and that's an added bonus. So yes, it's great to try new things, but it's even better when you find people who naturally share the same passions you do, as it makes a perfect environment for a friendship to develop.

So, to sum it up, don't start smoking just to meet new people; make better choices! Do try new things, such as a new club, a new sport, or a new hobby, and give the people there a chance. It's good to step outside of your comfort zone, and you may even find you're fantastic at something like fencing! This is a great way to make new friends.

> Learning how to read social situations can really help you when trying to meet new people. A common mistake often made is walking into an already established group of friends and trying to "own it" without understanding how the group operates. Usually, each person in a group has a role they play, such as the loud one, the quiet one, the funny one, and so on. If you don't respect the group dynamics, you might find that some people resent you. However, if you observe the group a little more before joining, this will definitely help.

This is where a little bit of emotional intelligence can play a huge role. One of my favorite examples of this is a playground situation in which a group of children are all playing with toy helicopters. One child who wants to join the game runs in and grabs one of the helicopters off another child, demanding to be allowed to play. This is an example of someone trying to own the situation, instead of making time to read it first. Naturally, the group doesn't appreciate this type of behaviour, and so the child is excluded straight away. A second child uses a different method, and instead of barging his way into the established game, he stands back and simply observes for a few minutes. He notices how the children involved are playing, he identifies who seems to be the leader of the group, and just observes them before making his move. When one child in the group drops his helicopter, the observing child sees it as his cue to run in, pick up the toy, and hand it back to the child playing with it. He smiles as he hands the toy over, and the other child accepts this as a kind gesture. The child who was observing makes a comment about loving helicopters and is then asked if he would like to play with the group.

▶ Think about how you choose to behave when interacting with others. Do you demand to be seen and accepted into a group straight away? Or do you observe patiently and slowly build up relationships through kind words and gestures? The fact of the matter is sometimes people don't have many friends because of their behaviour. So, my advice is to take time to reflect on the choice of behaviour you have made, or make daily, and ask yourself *How useful it is? Is it helpful?*

Remember, we like people who are like ourselves, and I'm not talking about our looks or ethnicity, but about our characteristics, beliefs, and values. I don't believe this changes very much as we grow older. When I look at my friendship circle now, there are very strong similarities among us all. My friends are quite strong personalities, they are funny, many are Irish, and so we *get* the same kind of things. They are kind and caring; they believe in family, in honesty, and in working hard for something you want. They are go-getters and are hilarious! Some of our values and beliefs are similar, others are different, but it all works well together.

KEY TAKEAWAYS FROM THIS CHAPTER:

❶

Remember, at the end of the day, people generally like others who are kind, considerate, and honest—things that absolutely anyone can choose to be. Once you've got these three things, you're on to being a winner.

❷

If you believe it's hard to make friends, it will be; it's as simple as that. Instead, hold the belief that you are able to make new friends easily.

❸

Take a chance and be the person who says hi first, because as much as they might want to speak to you, too, quite often we have to go first.

"When it comes to your friendship group, make it quality over quantity every time."

— LINDA BONNAR

12 I don't like going to parties, but then I feel left out when it's all my friends talk about.

Parties aren't all fun and games for everyone. For some people, they can be a nightmare. And if you feel like this, it can be even more irritating when someone asks you "Why?" or "What's wrong with you? It's just a party". It's rarely just about the party. You might start to feel left out as a result of the conversations that take place before and after the party.

▶ My first thought on this would be to get to the root of the issue because there is something there that's causing you to feel like this. What is it specifically about being at a party that you don't like?

⏸ And we work our way through that by asking how is this a problem for you?

And how is the problem you identified above a problem for you?

You can spend a few minutes on this asking yourself *How is this a problem for me?* This will help you get to the bottom of the issue. I'm not going to mind-read here, but the reasons could be anything from disliking being in a crowd to not knowing how to handle certain situations when you feel out of your comfort zone. You are the only one who can pinpoint what that issue is; I can only help you deal with it.

⏪ It might look something like this:

Let's say that this person doesn't like parties because of what they've experienced at parties they've already been to, and it's just not sat well with them. Imagine that they've been to two house parties at the same house when the parents were away. They didn't enjoy the first one but felt pressured into going a second time, and they were told "It will be different this time", but it wasn't. So naturally the experience they've had is going to have an effect on them. Remember that often we take one experience and paint others with the same brush, or we presume because it's happened once that it will happen again. If we apply the questions it might read something like this:

Q: What is it specifically about being at a party that makes you feel uncomfortable?
A: My friends just seem to get really drunk and annoying!
Q: And how is this a problem for you?
A: I don't agree with drinking, and I see the consequences of it. I just get this terrible feeling something awful will happen to my friends, like what happened at that last house party, that was a mess! I try to warn them, but they don't listen. I don't think it's safe.

We don't have to delve further into this to see that this person has seen some consequences of young people drinking, and the bottom line is they feel it's not safe, so something obviously isn't sitting well with this person.

⏩ If you're in this situation, what can you do?

1. Remember you've always got choices. If you would like to be at the party so you can at least discuss it afterwards and feel part of the group, you could ask yourself *What do I need to accept about this situation so I can be with my friends/talk about it with my friends afterwards?* or *Is there anything I can do to adapt to the situation better? Can I look at the positives instead of the negatives of the situation?* If you don't enjoy parties because you don't feel confident in talking to new people, have a read through Chapter 11 or Chapter 18 in this section

to get some tips on how to overcome this aspect. Or if you're not feeling very self-confident, try the Superman/Superwoman pose from Chapter 1 in Part 1, too.

2. Speak to your friends regarding what is specifically bothering you about the party situation. Get it out in the open and see if they feel the same about it or can help you through it.

3. However, if it's a situation you're really not comfortable with, then that's something else. If being in the situation at the party is going against your values or your beliefs, which it could very well do, then it's not going to sit well with you regardless of what you do!

4. For example, if you don't agree with drinking alcohol at a certain age, but there's alcohol freely available at a party, and people are getting drunk and not making great choices, then that's going against something you believe in, and you won't be happy being a part of it. Perhaps the house is being trashed at this party, and if you feel it's disrespectful, then you won't be comfortable either. Any situation that goes against your values or beliefs is, of course, going to make you feel uncomfortable.

5. Just because you haven't been at the party doesn't mean you have to be left out of the conversation. Your friends are not deliberately excluding you, so what efforts can you make to get involved in the conversation?

Could it be that if you show more interest in the conversation that you'll be included in it more, regardless of the fact you weren't at the party? Think about it logically, because there will be many times you won't share particular experiences with your friends, but you will still want to feel involved in their lives.

6. Now think about things you could do, or steps you could take, to feel more included in your friendship group. You don't like going to parties; that's fine, so could you organize something yourself for your friends to do?

7. Can you gear some conversations towards things you do enjoy or events you all have participated in together?

Sometimes there are things in life we just have to accept. If people in your friendship group develop new interests, it doesn't mean you have to follow suit, especially if it's going to make you incredibly uncomfortable. Your values and beliefs are important, and you already know what happens when you go against them.

KEY TAKEAWAYS FROM THIS CHAPTER:

❶

Stepping outside of our comfort zones can be a good thing when it encourages us to grow personally, because it helps us to develop our inner strength. But only you can figure out that line between a challenging level of discomfort and being in a situation where you feel your values are being disrespected.

❷

Find out what it is specifically that you don't like the situation and then look at the choices you have of dealing with it. What can you accept? How could you adapt to the situation?

❸

Taking the Superman/Superwoman pose is a great technique for a bit of instant confidence at social gatherings. Stand up straight with your feet slightly apart, elbows bent and hands on your hips. Head up, look ahead, and smile.

"The person who follows the crowd will usually go no further than the crowd."

ALBERT EINSTEIN

13 Compared to my friends, I feel fat and unattractive. I've started dieting but can't seem to stop.

Whether it's been walking around shopping malls, doing break-time duty as a teacher, or just sitting on public transport, the number of times I've overheard conversations or comments from groups of young people about weight loss, their looks, and dieting is incredible. From the talks of desires to be thin and the comparisons to others, to the "how-to" tips and tricks of it all, the pride at how long they can go without food and the incessant calorie counting, it just saddens me so much. What really concerns me about this chapter heading is that the person no longer seems to be in control of their food intake, and that's a problem. Contrary to popular belief, eating disorders don't just affect girls or young women, and they're not "phases" or "lifestyle choices"; they are serious mental disorders which affect people physically and psychologically and in serious cases, left untreated, can result in death. Before we carry on, I cannot stress how important it is that an eating disorder must be treated by a medical professional; sometimes a team of medical professionals is required depending on the individual's situation.

What can you do?

1. If you're concerned that you have an eating disorder yourself, the first thing you need to do is recognise that there is a problem. Symptoms like being primarily focused on weight loss and food control are key indicators, extreme preoccupation with body shape and size, developing food rituals, or being uncomfortable eating around others are also some other symptoms.
2. Accept that there is a problem. Many of us don't like to admit there's a problem or that we're losing control in a certain area of our lives. Remember there is no shame in admitting there is something wrong; it's extremely brave and courageous.
3. Get professional help as soon as possible. If you're unsure where to go or who to ask, start with a trusted adult. If you're lucky enough to have a school

counsellor, speak to them, as they'll be able to begin to provide you with the support you need to begin your recovery.
4. Accept that recovery will take some time. People recover from eating disorders at different rates, for a variety of reasons. Know your recovery will be individual for you and avoid comparing your recovery to anyone else's.

▶ What can you do if you're worried about a friend?

1. If you're worried about someone, then the best thing you can do is say something to them; don't ignore it and hope that it will go away or hope that someone else will say something. When you speak to the person in question, let them know that your concern comes from a good place and that you choosing to approach the subject with them isn't an attack on them at all.
2. If you're worried about how the other person might react, or you think they might cut you off and not let you finish, you could think about expressing your concerns and fears in a letter. Follow up the letter with a conversation. During the conversation, do your very best to use "I" statements, like "I have become very concerned because I've noticed . . ." or "I am worried about you . . ."
3. The person's reaction might not be the one you're hoping for. Be prepared for denial, anger, shouting, frustration, hurt, upset, tears, maybe even all of the above and more. None of these are unusual reactions.
4. It can be incredibly frustrating to support someone with an eating disorder. You might feel angry because it's really hard to understand why someone would choose to do such things to their body, and that's okay. We're not all meant to understand these things, and there's nothing wrong with admitting that either. If you're currently in this position with someone you care about, you could use this kind of statement: "I'm concerned about you. I don't exactly understand what you're going through, but I want you to know I'm always here to listen if you want to talk, and I'll support you in whatever way I can".

⏸ My own experience

I had no idea what to expect when I started my recovery process, and in hindsight, I wish I had the strength and the courage to put my hand up and say I needed help a lot earlier than I did. Even though I had lots of support, there were times when I felt incredibly alone because I knew there were very few people who could understand what I was going through. As part of my recovery, I had individual sessions with a psychiatrist to help me deal with the eating disorder, I was asked to keep a food journal, and I was also prescribed medication for the anxiety and depression I was experiencing, too. The medication definitely helped to stabilize my mood, and being able to have open and honest discussions with a professional about what I was experiencing was also really helpful.

While everything I did as part of my recovery played a role, I know now that two of the biggest things that helped me take control of the eating disorder was the work that I did with my doctor on learning to manage my thoughts and changing the beliefs I had about food and my physical appearance. Through this work, I realised how vicious my own thinking pattern was, and how quickly it would spiral out of control making me feel guilty, ashamed, and yes, fat. Slowly but surely, I began working to replace these automatic negative thoughts with more constructive thoughts. I realised I had a set of beliefs around food and my appearance that were hindering my whole recovery. I believed I was fat. I believed that in order to be considered "pretty", I had to be thin. I believed that being thin was a measure of my personal success, and I believed that being thinner would make me happier. How could I even begin to feel confident about myself with these beliefs? I knew they had to change.

My journey to recovery most certainly didn't happen overnight. It's been a long process, but it's all been worth it, too, because I firmly believe it's made me the stronger person I am right now. Today, I make sure that I reward my body for what it has done instead of how I used to punish it for what I'd eaten. I've accepted myself for who I am, I'm much more in control of my mind and the thoughts I allow to take center stage in my head. I have a set of strong, constructive beliefs which continually help me move forward to be the best version of myself, and I surround myself with amazing, positive people who support me and my ambitious goals!

Recovery from an eating disorder of any kind is most certainly possible, but the change all begins with you first.

KEY TAKEAWAYS FROM THIS CHAPTER:

❶

Comparing yourself to others is not a useful strategy for improving your self-esteem or self-confidence. Likewise, never rely on a weighing scale or measuring tape to measure your self-worth. There's only one of you; embrace it.

❷

Work on developing a more positive body image by reminding yourself of all that your body can do and reward it for its achievements instead of punishing it through restrictive diets.

❸

Remember that beauty is a state of mind, not a state of your body; when you accept yourself, you'll always appear naturally beautiful to those around you.

"Take care of your body. It's the only place you have to live."

— JIM ROHN

14 I feel my friends don't care about me anymore.

On a bad day, we might well feel like certain friends don't care about us anymore. We also need to be very realistic and see that this isn't always the actual fact of the matter. Remember: feelings are not facts.

> My first question for you to think about in this situation is *Where is your evidence to support these feelings?* Bear in mind that when we believe something to be true, we end up looking for evidence to support that belief. This is why, in these situations, I recommend talking it through with someone else who can challenge you if the evidence you give seems a bit flimsy. Perhaps have them ask you the questions. So, where is your evidence to support your statement?

At this stage, if you have skipped Part 1 of this book, I'm going to encourage you to read Chapter 2 in particular, which investigates different thinking errors and helps you to learn how to begin replacing negative thoughts with more constructive thoughts. Now that you've looked at the evidence you've gathered to support your statement, how would you measure the strength of this evidence? Would you have any reason to question it at all?

I am inviting you to evaluate the statement you are making, and question how rational it is, by considering the evidence. When there's emotion involved, it can be very hard to look at things rationally. Let's look at the situation with a wider lens. Is there anything currently going on inside your friendship group that could have encouraged you to think or feel this way?

Is there anything going on outside of your friendship group at the moment that's encouraging you to think or feel this way about your friends?

The reason I ask this question is that quite often when something is bothering us, it can affect us in many different ways. For example, if we are feeling low about ourselves, then sometimes we create random "if/then" consequences such as *If I don't do well in this test, then it means I'm rubbish at math*, or *If my friends are a bit quiet with me, then this means they don't care about me.* You might not sleep very well or eat very well when something is on your mind, and your concentration will probably be off too. Moreover, when one part of our life isn't going very well, we tend to blame ourselves and question our self-worth. And when things don't go the way we want them to, it's easy to fall into the "I'm not good enough" vicious circle. Be aware of that circle, because it's a negative one, and it's full of irrational thinking.

By now you either have some reliable evidence to support your claim, or you've realized that your claim isn't fully justified. Perhaps you've pinpointed that you've been a bit down on yourself lately, and so you've assumed your friends don't really care about you even though there is no real evidence.

▶ What can you do?

Instead of allowing this worry to swim around in your mind, get it out of your head. What stops you from asking your friends straight out if something has changed in your relationship? You'll never know unless you ask and find out. A direct question stops the mind-reading hamster wheel and allows you to get focused on the real facts, because feelings are not facts! Wonder where you've heard that before, eh?!

And if your friends say that things have changed between you and them? Well, if this is the case, then obviously it's not very nice, and it's most definitely not nice to hear. But we only have control over our own reactions, we can't control how other people react to us. Yes, you could begin to change yourself so that these other people like you more, but at what cost? And even if you did change yourself to please them, what's to say that they won't change again, and then what will you do? Change is the one thing in life that is guaranteed to happen, and this includes in friendships too. You can choose to pursue a friendship that probably won't serve or help you very much in life, or you can accept that perhaps the friendship has run its course. A very wise lady once said to me, "Friendships can work like seasons: they come and they go. Sometimes they bring pleasant experiences, and sometimes they leave us feeling uncomfortable, but whatever they do, there is always something to be learned from them". I do believe that people are meant to come into your life for a particular reason, and looking at what we can learn from them will make accepting this change a lot easier.

KEY TAKEAWAYS FROM THIS CHAPTER:

❶

Feelings are fleeting; they come and go and sometimes they don't tell us the truth. If you're feeling an uncomfortable emotion, don't ignore it, check it out, and be open to the possibility that it might not be accurate.

❷

Address the question that's on your mind—asking questions doesn't always mean you'll get the answers you want, but it's definitely better than having the unanswered questions swimming around in your head.

❸

Accept that people change: we change and our relationships with people will change, too. Change is the one constant thing in life.

"A friend who listens and understands your tears is much more valuable than a lot of friends who only know your smile."

UNKNOWN

15. I'm concerned that my friend might be depressed, and I don't know what to do.

It's perfectly normal for us to feel sad from time to time. Sadness is a natural reaction to an upsetting or stressful situation, which I think it's fair to say we all experience at some stage in our lives. And while most of us will recognize sadness as a feeling that comes and goes, it's when this sadness stays with us for a particularly long time, and affects our day-to-day lives, that it becomes something more serious. Depression is more than just feeling sad or feeling a bit down; it's a prolonged feeling of sadness. Depression is a mental illness, and as a result, must be taken seriously and treated by a medical professional.

> One of the things I admire about this person's statement is that they are concerned. They have noticed changes in a friend's behaviour or attitude and they want to help. If you, as a friend, have noticed changes in a friend's behaviour, then it's likely there is something up. Have a look at the list of symptoms below and then ask yourself if any of them sound familiar when you think about your friend.

- Not wanting to do things that you previously enjoyed
- Not wanting to meet up with friends, avoiding situations, or becoming withdrawn
- Sleeping more or less than normal (for you/your friend)
- Eating more or less than normal (for you/your friend)
- Feeling irritable, upset, miserable, or lonely
- Being self-critical
- Feeling hopeless
- Maybe wanting to self-harm
- Feeling tired and not having any energy
- Experiencing problems with thinking, focus, concentration, creativity, and the ability to make decisions most days

This is similar to Chapter 13 on eating disorders in that concerns like this do need to be handled in a sensitive manner. Have a look back over that chapter and see if the material there proves useful in this situation, too. Everyone is different, so I don't feel there's a set textbook guide to broaching this subject with someone. But as I've said already, if you are concerned or worried about someone, SAY SOMETHING.

If someone has chosen to speak to you about something like depression, or any mental illness for that matter, treat it seriously and give them your full attention. It's important to point out here that sometimes you don't have to say anything at all. Sometimes being the person who simply listens, without judgment, is the most important role you can play. Supporting someone with any form of mental illness can be very tough, so you need to make sure you've got a support network in place, too. Depression is a very common mental illness affecting approximately one in four people around the world. It doesn't discriminate against gender, age, race, or religion and can affect anyone at any point in their lives. While this chapter focuses on supporting a friend in particular, if you're concerned that you may be depressed, it's important that you speak to an adult and get professional help as soon as possible, because you are not alone and depression is treatable.

Below is a list of some good and not-so-good things you can do when wanting to help.

Good idea	Not such a good idea
Speak to someone in authority, or offer to accompany the person if they need some support in seeing a school counsellor, doctor, or teacher.	Promise you won't tell anyone. If the person shares something with you that puts them at risk, you have a duty of care to report it to someone who can help.
Show your concern. Give the person your time to hear them out when possible.	Tell the person they're "not normal". They feel pretty terrible as it is, so they don't need anyone else adding to these feelings.
Listen without any judgment at all. Just listen to hear what is being said and notice how it's being said.	Begin a reply with "At least", e.g., "At least you're doing really well in school."

Good idea	Not such a good idea
Try to empathize with the person or their experience. It makes people feel less abnormal.	Ignore the issue and hope that someone else will do something to help.
Respect that it's probably taken a lot for this person to speak about what they are going through.	

KEY TAKEAWAYS FROM THIS CHAPTER:

❶

Depression is more than feeling sad or down about something for a day or two, and while some causes of depression might be preventable like how you choose to look after yourself, other causes, like genetic factors, are not.

❷

If you're worried about someone, then say something, keeping in mind that as a young adult, you are not expected to have the answers or to support your friend like an adult or medical professional.

❸

People often worry about saying the wrong thing to someone battling depression, and that's okay. Sometimes the best thing we can do is to offer to be there, to listen without judgment.

"One in four people like me have a mental health problem. Many more people have a problem with that."

STEPHEN FRY

16 My friend is in a toxic and abusive relationship.

Our relationships need to be good relationships. This means they need to be built on trust and there need to be mutual respect and support, love and honesty. Any relationship which is not built on a foundation of respect is not a good relationship, full stop.

Unfortunately, we can sometimes end up in negative relationships that are toxic or abusive. It's important that you know the characteristics of these relationships so you can recognise them and avoid them.

Toxic relationships will often consist of the following:

1. Constant judgment or criticism
2. Placing blame on others or lack of accountability for behaviours
3. Lack of consideration for the other person; a "what's in it for me" type of attitude
4. Constant negativity
5. Attempts to control the other person, anger, and jealousy

How can you leave a toxic relationship?

1. Be honest about the relationship and see it for what it really is. If you recognise that it's toxic, then staying in it is not helpful. Sometimes when it comes to making the decision to leave a toxic relationship, we feel guilty or feel we "should" stay in it as if we owe the other person something.
2. Be honest and express your feelings about the relationship. When something doesn't feel right, do your best to put a name on that feeling so you can deal with it in the appropriate way for you.
3. Surround yourself with positive people for support.
4. Reward yourself for taking the steps to remove yourself from a relationship that no longer serves you.

5. Avoid speaking ill of the other person when you disconnect from them—it doesn't help you. If ever asked about them, you can simply say you've not seen them in some time.

Abusive relationships can take all shapes and forms. It could involve physical, emotional, or verbal abuse. We might also think abusive relationships are just pertinent to adults, but young people can also be susceptible to them. Abuse is often an attempt to gain power over the other. Abusive relationships are NEVER okay, and I mean NEVER.

Let's look at this from the perspective of a boyfriend/girlfriend relationship. It might be the kind of thing you have seen in the movies, where the guy turns controlling on the girl and gets jealous, not allowing her to talk to other guys or have other male friends. We sit there watching the story unfold, desperately hoping she will finally have a wake-up call and realize he won't change, and that staying with him, hoping he will change, is not a good move. The good thing is that at the end, we can switch the movie off and that's it. However, what if the girl in the movie is your friend? Or what if she's you?

Let's look at this from two perspectives, the first one being the friend scenario. The difficulty here is that often your friend might not see, or maybe doesn't want to see, what is really going on. It can appear like they are blinkered. So, as their friend, you see the abuse taking place, you hear the name-calling or the demands, and you see how this affects your friend, but it's almost like you are paralyzed to do anything about it. However, even though it might feel like that, there are some things you can do.

1. Be honest and open with your friend, and tell them exactly what you see going on. Make it very clear, and use "I" statements. For example, "I've seen that . . ." Be careful not to mind-read, or generalize with statements like "I know what is being said to you . . ." or "This is just typical of guys like that!"
2. Continually show your concern. Your friend might be very aware that they are not in a healthy relationship but might have no idea what to do about it, or might also be terrified to do something about it. Remember, fear is often what keeps someone in an abusive relationship. Be prepared for them to tell you to get lost! You might be told to keep your nose out of it, or told you have

no idea what's going on. Tell your friend you are worried, concerned for their safety and their emotional and mental health.

3. Listen, without judgment, to what your friend has to say. You may want to fix the issue, but that's not your role. If your friend has chosen to speak to you about what they are going through, then please listen. Sometimes you might even respond with a nod, and a simple, "I hear what you are saying." If your friend fears that they are going to be judged, then there's a high chance they'll shut down and say nothing.

4. You could ask your friend if they are willing to have an open conversation with you about this, where there is no judgment involved. HelpGuide.org have a section on abusive relationships, and you can use some questions from there, such as:
    - Do you ever feel afraid of your boyfriend/girlfriend?
    - Does your boyfriend/girlfriend ever put you down or belittle you?
    - Do you avoid certain topics out of fear of angering your boyfriend/girlfriend?
    - Do you feel that you can't do anything right for your boyfriend/girlfriend?
    - Does your boyfriend/girlfriend act excessively jealous?

Remember that as a young person, you are not expected to have all the answers, and whenever possible, it's important to speak to a trusted adult, too. Again, be prepared for your friend to be angry if you do speak to someone. They might feel betrayed, but in the long run, they will see that you've spoken to someone out of concern and not malice. Sometimes it might feel like you aren't doing enough for your friend, but trust me, by supporting, listening, and being there for them, you are doing everything you can, and it will be remembered.

KEY TAKEAWAYS FROM THIS CHAPTER:

❶

Having healthy relationships is a key component to our overall happiness and well-being. Healthy relationships are those in which we feel respected, valued and safe. Toxic relationships are characterized by constant negativity, judgment, and criticism. Abusive relationships are never healthy and are detrimental to our physical, emotional and mental well-being.

❷

No one will treat you with love and respect unless you do so for yourself first.

❸

To help you disconnect from a toxic person try the following technique: Point to yourself with both hands and say, "I'm me." Then imagining the other person standing in front of you, point to them with both hands and say, "You're you." Then, making cutting or finishing gestures with both hands across your body, say, "We're different." This helps your brain to disconnect from the other person.

"Respect yourself enough to walk away from anything that no longer serves you, grows you, or makes you happy."

ROBERT TEW

17 I'm not sure if I'm jealous or envious of my friends, but either way, it's not a nice feeling. How can I stop it?

In today's society, where we're constantly bombarded with other people's amazing highlight reels on social media, it's very easy for envy to rear its not-very-pretty head. I think most of us have fallen victim to this at some point or another where we've longed for something someone else has.

Let's start with differentiating between envy and jealousy before we look at how to deal with them. Envy is basically wanting something that someone else has and jealousy is when you worry someone else will take what you have. While they are different emotions, sometimes they do travel together, and sometimes they bring along other uncomfortable emotions like anger, guilt, and shame to the party, too. I've been envious of people who have their own horse (actually, I still am, who am I kidding?!), of runners with super-quick running times, and of houses with big gardens. But have these desires ever had a negative impact on my behaviours? No, because I don't allow them to—simple. However, like many of our emotions, if we don't learn to control them, they can prompt us to behave in a way we'll end up regretting. We need to first of all recognise the emotions present and then learn to manage them appropriately.

> When you take the above definitions into account, do you think you're dealing with envy or jealousy in your situation?

▶ Okay, let's look at where we can begin.

Let's look at a few coaching questions to help us deal with this. I've given some examples to help you along the way, too.

1. Can you pinpoint what it is that stirs up these unwanted feelings of envy or jealousy inside you?
   Example: *Yes, I'm envious of my friends' wealth. They get whatever they want and I don't.*
   Example: *Yes, I'm jealous of this one girl in my class. I know she's trying to take my best friend away from me.*
   Your answer:

2. How would you like to be reacting instead?
   Example: *I'd like to just appreciate what I have without creating comparisons to what someone else has in their life.*
   Example: *I'd like to think that she's a nice person and let that be it.*
   Your answer:

3. How would this more constructive reaction help you?
   Example: *It would stop that nasty voice in my head that starts talking when my friends tell me about their amazing, expensive holidays, for a start.*
   Example: *If I thought she was a nice person, I'd be so much nicer to her, but instead I feel like I'm defensive around her.*
   Your answer:

4. What would you need to stop doing in order to create this more positive response/reaction?
   Example: *I would need to stop comparing my family's wealth to my friends'.*
   Example: *I would need to stop presuming she's trying to take my friend away. I've just realised I'm mind-reading here; I have no evidence for my accusation.*
   Your answer:

5. What would you have to start doing in order to have this more construction reaction?

   Example: *Appreciate what we do have at home, and realise how different my parents' jobs are compared to my friends' parents. We can't afford the stuff they have.*

   Example: *Checking for evidence when those little negative voices pop into my head for a start!*

   Your answer:

Some people find answering a few coaching questions like these really helpful in creating solutions to the problem.

Let's take a look at some tips you can use to deal with envy:

1. Remember, envy is an emotion, and all emotions are common. It's okay to feel envious from time to time, so let go of any self-judgment and let your inner critic know you're in control!
2. All emotions are useful in some context, even uncomfortable emotions, e.g., anger, can motivate us to say what's on our minds. How can you put feelings of envy to good use? What could it motivate you to do?
3. Use feelings of envy as a sign to compliment someone and create an even better relationship with them. If I feel envious about someone having a super quick running time, instead of getting frustrated with my own running, I can compliment their efforts, ask them for some running tips, etc.

Now let's look at some ways of managing jealousy:

1. If jealousy is a reaction to a thought or a belief you have, we firstly need to become aware of these so that we can begin working to replace them with more constructive thoughts and beliefs, e.g., *I think that he's trying to take my girlfriend from me*, or *I believe that people cannot be faithful in relationships* are not conducive to healthy relationships. You could see how this type of thought or this type of belief could easily spur on the hamster wheel of negative thoughts. By being aware and replacing them, we can stop that cycle.

2. Jealousy can arise from a feeling of being threatened, but remember that feelings are not facts, so get a realistic view of the situation; get facts and evidence.
3. Jealousy can arise from low self-esteem or self-confidence. Focus on all that you have, all of your skills, your successes and achievements; knowing your own self-worth will reduce feelings of jealousy.
4. If jealousy arises within a relationship, speak about how you are feeling in a calm, direct, and rational manner. Use "I have seen . . . and this has caused me to feel . . ." or "When I heard . . . I felt . . ."

KEY TAKEAWAYS FROM THIS CHAPTER:

❶

Envy is a very common emotion to experience, especially when someone else has something we want or has succeeded in a way we'd like to. Jealousy most typically shows up when we feel threatened by a third person, and fear losing something or someone.

❷

Identify the negative thought that is feeding your feelings of envy and feed it with a whole list of things you're grateful for instead; reduce envy with gratitude.

❸

Jealousy can be triggered by an irrational thought, so quiet it with your rational thoughts and a calm voice.

"Feelings are much like waves, we can't stop them from coming, but we can choose which one to surf."

JONATAN MÅRTENSSON

18) My friends think I'm really shy, when in fact I'm terrified I'll say the wrong thing to someone I've just met.

Were you ever told as a very young child to "just go and make friends" with some of the other children in the playground or when you were on holidays with your family somewhere? Sometimes parents say it to their children like there's nothing to it at all, like it's a Nike advert and we should all just do it! While some people appear to just walk into a room and have people naturally flock to them, many of us become suddenly quite awkward, or even anxious, around people we've not met before. Why? Simply because we want people to like us. We want to fit in and be accepted, and we might even want to be popular. So instead of getting tongue-tied or saying something inappropriate, let's have a look at a few things you can do.

⏸ Think of someone you know who is good with other people and has many friends. What makes them this way? What do they do? How do they behave around others? Remember that behaviours can be learned. I'm not saying to start imitating them or dressing like them, but observe what it is that makes them good socially. Are they the kind of person who can just walk right into a group and be accepted? If they can, it's probably because they've developed good social awareness. They've learned to read the situation and time things well.

⏸ Think for a moment about certain things you do in social situations. What kinds of responses do you tend to get?

My point here is that we may have to learn how to interact with others just as if it were a type of skill. Make no mistake at all that how we deal with others is a skill—a social skill—and one that we get better at with practice. In developing this skill, I'm going to be referring to emotional intelligence (EI). I make reference to

EI at various points in the book, but for now, we'll focus on it in terms of being self-aware and being sensitive to those around us.

First, here's what not to do. Have you ever seen someone try to come into a group and take the role of "leader" right away? Or change the subject to what they want to talk about, without discussion, or without figuring out what the group dynamics are? How does it usually end up for that person? Not very good, right? And unfortunately, this is what some of us do when we meet a new group of people first: we charge in! Maybe you've seen people who try to draw attention to themselves right away by creating some type of conflict, or constantly talk about their opinions without taking the opinions of others into account. Yes, the positive intention in this behaviour is usually the hope that people will like them, but it doesn't always end up that way. So, if we're not getting the results we want in life, we need to change something.

Here's another option that might work better: People are accepted more quickly into groups when they don't try and take over, but when they respect the current situation, even if they don't like it very much. They respect the boundaries that the group has established. So, the best idea is to show an interest in a group of people while respecting the roles the people play in that group. A bad idea is trying to take over the group for yourself and become the ring leader, without knowing who's who.

What can you do?

1. How about watching and observing first? There's nothing wrong with being shy or being "the shy one" in the group, as this gives you plenty of time to observe others and what they do. Then break this mould gradually and practice your social skills.
2. A great way to break the ice and speak to new people is to start by finding some common ground between you and them. We like people who are like ourselves. Again, we're not talking about imitating a person or lying about what hobbies you have, but maybe you've got a love of sports in common, a place you've recently visited, or perhaps you're both the oldest in the family.

3. Compliment the person. It's a great icebreaker, and we all love a compliment. Plus, the more you give, the more you get! You could say something like "I really like your shirt", or "That color really suits you", or "You played a great game out there today". Just make sure it's a genuine compliment and you really mean it.

4. If you find you don't have much in common with the person, then ask them what they do enjoy doing, because people LOVE talking about themselves. Are you worried about asking the wrong question, especially if it's a topic you don't know a lot about? Then keep it simple with something like "I don't know a lot about X, how did you develop an interest in it?" or "What do you enjoy about it?"

5. Don't force it. There's nothing worse than someone who is fake. Accept that you won't get on well with everyone, and it's simply easier when people like you for who you are and not for who they want you to be.

6. Smile when you meet new people. Smiling puts people at ease, it makes you seem more approachable, and everyone looks better when they smile! Your body language says a lot about you and can reveal how you feel about the person you're talking to.

7. Becoming socially aware also means we tune in more to other people's feelings, and this is where empathy comes into play. There is a fine—but incredibly important—line between empathy and sympathy. If someone has lost their pet, then we show sympathy by saying we're sorry for their loss. Empathy is being able to put yourself in someone else's shoes and walk around in them. "I know how awful this is", "I understand what you're going through", "I'm here for you" are the kinds of things we say when we are empathetic. Some people feel they can't show empathy if they've never been through the experience the other person is going through, but you can still show you care with a response like, "I'm sorry you're experiencing this. I've no idea how hurt you must feel right now, but please know I'm here to support you, even if you just want someone to listen to you".

8. Lastly, remember that it's not a competition. While it's great to find or build common ground with people you've just met, you don't need to get one up on them. If you find yourself saying "I do that, too", or "I, I, I . . .", create a more mutual space by highlighting things you've both done. For example,

"WE'VE been to many of the same places", "WE'VE got a lot in common", "WE seem to like the same music".

9. Keep in mind that social situations are sometimes a challenge for adults as well, trust me! Walking into a room full of people who all seem to know each other can be incredibly daunting, and it's even worse when they're all wearing suits. There have been hundreds of times when I've met someone new, said something, saw the look on their faces, and immediately thought, *GET ME OUT OF HERE!* We've all had those times when you actually do wish someone would set off the fire alarm so you could run out of the building, never to see that person again. But you deal with it, and you move on, and that's what all of this is really about: moving on. Put these things down to experience and learn from them; that's the best thing you can do.

KEY TAKEAWAYS FROM THIS CHAPTER:

❶

Being able to speak to new people you meet is a skill, and like any skill, the more you practice it, the easier it gets, and the better you get at it. It's perfectly fine not to know what to say all the time. Plus, it's good emotional intelligence to sometimes stand back and observe before we open our mouths.

❷

Take small steps first, like saying hello to new people at your school or in your local area. Keep in mind that sometimes people are just as nervous about "going first", so be courageous and take that first step.

❸

Ask open-ended questions which encourage the other person/people to express their opinions or views and then you can use their responses to carry on the conversation.

"You can make more friends in two months by becoming interested in other people than you can in two years by trying to get other people interested in you."

DALE CARNEGIE

19 I feel pressured into doing things in my friendship group that I'm just not comfortable with.

You'd be surprised to know how much I learned about young people while I was getting my research together for this book. I was surprised that this issue was highlighted by quite a few of the young men who helped me with my research, and not just girls. I was told a lot about different "initiation processes" that take place in some secondary schools, and honestly, I was quite perturbed by some of them. One of the things I mentioned in the earlier chapters was our need to feel that we belong and that we are a part of something bigger, which is a very strong human desire. There are a number of things we do each day in the hope that they will win us some admiration or acknowledgement from people we'd like to be associated with. The bottom line is that we want to belong.

Now usually this need to belong results in harmless stuff, such as saying we like a particular band in an attempt to fit in with a group. But what happens when your group begins to pressure you into things that go against your values or beliefs, such as experimenting with illegal substances or doing something else that is illegal? What do you do then? You want to be a part of the group, you want these people to like you and to think that you are "someone". You might even fancy a member of the group and see this as your way to build a closer relationship with that person. You don't want to be left out, so what can you do? Honestly, this is where it gets hard. If it were easy, I wouldn't be writing this chapter.

As an adult, it's hard to say no to certain things, so work on developing your inner strength now and work on this inner strength like it's a muscle. Then, like any muscle, the more you exercise it, the stronger it gets. But you've got to work it. My advice is to start with saying no to small things. This doesn't mean that you become rude or cheeky, but you simply begin to develop your independence, self-respect and self-confidence. If it's a group that's putting pressure on you, how about you begin to step away from the group when it suits you to do so? Think of three small things you can say no to this week to begin working your inner strength muscle.

⏸ 1.

2.

3.

Can you think of any bigger things that are coming up in the near future that you'd like to be able to say no to?

What will saying no these things do for you?

Be true to yourself and learn that sometimes it is perfectly fine to say no to something so you can do something that's more important to you. The more you practice taking these steps, the stronger this inner strength muscle gets, and the less surprised people are when you do turn down an offer. Your friends will eventually come to acknowledge and respect that this is who you are. Someone not easily led, someone who is happy to stand on their own and do what they want.

⏩ What can you do if the pressure continues?

Is there anything you can do to avoid it? Can you arrange to do something else? What else can you say if saying no just doesn't get people off your case? How about something like "I'm not sure why you can't accept no for an answer", or "Why the need to keep pushing this?" Being armed with these kinds of statements allows you to be seen as someone who is strong-minded.

At the end of the day, could your time be better spent with people who respect your decisions and don't pressure you? And if the answer is yes, then you know you've got another bit of work to do!

KEY TAKEAWAYS FROM THIS CHAPTER:

❶

While it's human nature to want to belong to groups and communities, if our values and beliefs are not being respected, we need to have the strength to stand alone. Saying no is a powerful thing to do for someone who respects their own boundaries.

❷

Practice saying no in an affirmative and confident manner in an environment you feel comfortable in first. The more you practice it, the more normal it will sound when you say it in other situations.

❸

If the pressure continues, back your no response up with a positive statement and not an extension or story. For example, if you're at a party and you're offered alcohol that you don't want, you could say "No thanks, I'm having a great time as it is" instead of "No, I don't drink because . . ."

"Be strong enough to stand alone, smart enough to know when you need help, and brave enough to ask for it."

— ZIAD K. ABDELNOUR

20) My friends have started to comment on my temper. I just can't seem to control it. I think I've got anger management issues.

As with all feelings, anger can be useful in certain circumstances. However, 90 percent of the time, anger is not useful at all and gets us into trouble. Anger is also dangerous because it's contagious. We rarely keep it just to ourselves. We carry it around and pass it on to others. Think about a time you've been angry or you've seen someone who was angry. They storm out of the room, slamming the door, maybe grunting at someone in the corridor instead of smiling or saying hello.

Learning to control anger in order to prevent it controlling us is a valuable skill. When we don't learn to control anger, it can spiral into a negative circle, leading to guilt, sadness, hurt, and yes, more anger.

Becoming more self-aware is really important when we're learning how to control any unwanted feeling. Put simply, when we talk about self-awareness in this part of the book, we're talking about our ability to recognize anger and to learn how to manage it so that it doesn't control us. Keep in mind that you can ALWAYS manage your feelings, you've just got to know how.

> There are certain triggers that bring about particular feelings. Certain things act as triggers for happiness, relaxation, sadness, and so on. What is it that triggers your anger?

Think about a time when you were angry. What was happening?

Was there anyone else involved?

It might be helpful to imagine the scene like it's a movie. You can rewind very slowly to see the buildup to this anger. As you do so, what do you notice? Where does it begin?

Finding the trigger is really important in order to manage your feelings. Once you know your triggers, you will have more control over the situation, and you can work on changing your reaction to something much more constructive. Let's take an example to work on and imagine that Tom thunders through the door at home, shouts at his mum, pushes his younger sibling out of the way, and runs up to his room, where he proceeds to slam the door and throw some stuff around. If we were to rewind the scene, we might have seen something like this:

Tom and his friends are hanging out and they start teasing him about liking a girl. It all starts off as a joke until something triggers Tom's anger inside. He's unsure of how to deal with it in a constructive way, so he takes it out on his friends by shouting at them and storming off. His friends are left confused. They were only trying to have a laugh with him. By the time he's in his room, Tom's feeling pretty embarrassed, and he knows he needs to put a stop to this, so he begins to find his trigger.

As I show you how to do this, we will look at it through Tom's eyes.

Step 1: Identify what was happening

I was sitting around with the lads chatting, and one of them got on my case about Katie. As soon as they mentioned her name, my heart started pounding, and I felt myself go bright red, and then I got really angry. I looked across the lunch hall and saw her. I smiled at her, but I'd swear she just smirked at me, then turned around laughing with all her girlfriends. This just made me worse! So, I stormed off.

Tom has begun to rewind the scene for himself to identify what it was that triggered this anger, and it appears that it was when the lads mentioned Katie, he describes why this triggered his anger below.

Step 2: How is this a problem for you?

Because I actually like Katie, but the lads don't know that yesterday I asked her out, and she said no. So now I feel embarrassed and rejected. I wish she'd said yes, or I wish I'd never even asked her. I feel stupid, and I'm so angry with myself for even asking her out in the first place. Being rejected by her just made me so angry. I was so hurt, who likes being rejected?

And there we can clearly see what triggered Tom's anger.

Step 3: By asking the question again you can dig a little further. How is you asking her out a problem?

It's a problem because I'm so angry with myself, and I'm angry with the lads, too. They should have known better; they know I like her.

Now let's look at some coaching questions I used that helped Tom to see things differently, quell his anger, and move on from the situation.

Me: So, if I've heard you right, the lads should have known that you asked her out even though you didn't tell them?
Tom: Well, yeah, they're my friends.
Me: Okay, are they also mind readers who know what's going on in your life if you don't tell them?
Tom: No, fair enough.
Me: What's a better reaction to choose in this situation?
Tom: Maybe if I had told the lads what happened, then they'd have said nothing about it.
Me: Okay. Anything else?
Tom: Or maybe if I didn't take the situation so seriously, I'd have been able to laugh about it instead of getting so angry.
Me: So, moving forward, what will you do?
Tom: I'll tell the lads what happened with her and be open with them.
Me: Excellent. Anything else?

Tom: I've realised that I took this really personally, and while it's still a bit annoying, it's really unlikely that I'll never be rejected again, right? So, time to put some of what we've talked about into place.

Me: That sounds good, Tom. Sounds like we've already got a coaching topic for our next session!

> You've always got a choice in how you react to things, and the better choice here is not to plague a person and beg them to go out with you—no way! Nor is the better choice to take your anger out on everyone else around you while you begin to question everything about yourself. Instead, you want to become aware of your own triggers and identify better ways of reacting in these situations. Let's look at the choices Tom now has.

1. He can ask himself what he's learned from the situation and use this to move on.
2. He can have a prepared comeback comment for if the lads mention Katie again. Something like, "Oh well, I'm glad she told me to my face" or, "Guess it's not meant to be". It's better to have something prepared to deal with it. "Bet the first girl Brad Pitt asked out in high school didn't say yes to him either".
3. Avoid falling into the habit of blaming others for your anger. Yes, maybe someone pushes your buttons a little too far, but you always have a choice in how you respond. I hear phrases like "She/he drives me mad a lot" when the reality of it is that no-one can drive you mad unless you give them the keys.

▶ Action steps for dealing with anger

Reading over the action steps we've already covered for dealing with stress in Chapter 9 may help, too, as there is some overlap.

1. Become aware of your own triggers. Recognize them, catch them, and become familiar with them so you're more in control of how you react to them. This is a great example of practicing self-awareness and self-management.

2. Get it out of your head and onto paper. Write about what is bothering you, write out better ways of dealing with the issue, and ask for help with this if you need it.
3. If you notice a pattern to your triggers or you find they're focused on a particular person, then it's time to do a little more work to find out what's really going on below the surface.
4. Control your breathing, and you will manage your thoughts better. As I said in the Chapter 9 on stress, deep breathing isn't just for hippies and people in robes! It's a very powerful tool, and one that can be practiced anywhere, at any time.
5. Develop a habit of having thinking time. Think before you speak, because you cannot take your words back, and words spoken in anger are rarely helpful, supportive, or caring. Some people find it helpful to use a traffic light system for this. Imagine a big red light that means you cannot speak. Take deep breaths to regain control, and imagine an orange light flashing, which encourages you to think of something more constructive to say. And then a green light gives you the go-ahead to speak. Remember these are skills, and skills all need practice.
6. When you're in a calmer state, speak using "I" statements such as "I feel . . .", "I'm hurt", "I'm sorry". "You" statements such as "You made me angry . . ." or "You shouldn't have said that" are accusatory and show that we're not taking responsibility for our own feelings, words, or actions.
7. Humor has its place in dealing with anger, just make sure it doesn't turn into sarcasm, as this is rarely helpful.
8. Take a time-out where possible to get away from the situation.
9. Incorporate a meditation app such as Headspace into your daily routine.
10. Incorporate more exercise into your day.
11. Become aware of certain thoughts that may be fueling anger. You could revisit Chapter 2 on tackling thinking errors to help you with this.

I used to be an incredibly angry person, and the smallest things would set me off. It could have been anything from a comment my dad made to thinking about something that had happened at school. When I eventually began to talk about the issues I was experiencing, the anger all came out. I was full of anger and blame. I seemed to be blaming everybody else for what had gone wrong in my life instead of taking responsibility for myself, my actions, and my reactions. My husband said to me one day, "You seem to be so angry, it's like you've got this bag full of anger from the past that you carry around with you, and you just won't put it down or deal with it. You need to learn to travel light and not let this stuff weigh you down". How very true.

I was still holding on to certain negative things from my past, and it only took one trigger to start the whole cycle of anger going again. Eventually I knew I had to deal with things rather than sweeping them under the carpet. You see, your brain has this way of doing certain things. You can sweep things under the carpet for a while, but as soon as your brain recognizes that you're in a place to finally handle these issues, it brings them back again.

How many times you want to keep sweeping things under that carpet is up to you. In dealing with my anger, I learned a lot about myself and my triggers. Becoming more aware of what sets you off can be very empowering. It gives you the option to choose better responses to these triggers so they become less powerful.

How did I learn to manage my anger? A combination of things, really, and nothing that happened magically overnight. I started practicing meditation with Headspace. I got things out of my head and onto paper more. This helped me begin to build rational ways of dealing with things. I accepted things and took responsibility for my actions. I stopped blaming others and learned to take a step back to look at things from other peoples' perspectives. I learned that people make the choices they feel are best for them at the time. So, when someone cuts me off at a junction now, instead of getting road rage, I've developed a better habit for me, which is to smile to myself and say, "He must have a really important meeting to get to".

KEY TAKEAWAYS FROM THIS CHAPTER:

❶

Like any uncomfortable emotion, there's no point in trying to ignore anger or suppress it. Instead, do your best to understand where the anger is coming from. Are you trying to gain control? To be heard? To fight an injustice? To gain power over someone else? Once you know why the anger is there, you can do something more constructive about it.

❷

Breathe, breathe, breathe. Breathe deeply and slowly from your belly. Inhale for a count of five, hold the breath for a count of five, and then slowly exhale for a count of five. Slow down your breathing and you'll slow down your thought process, allowing you to gain control.

❸

Create a "calm and relaxed" scene for yourself that you can use anytime you feel yourself getting angry. Focus on all the details of your calm and relaxed scene so your focus cannot be on the anger.

"Anger doesn't solve anything. It builds nothing, but it can destroy everything."

UNKNOWN

School

The Challenges Dealt With In PART 3

21. I just can't seem to focus in school.

22. I'm not getting good grades and my parents aren't happy about it.

23. I can't get motivated to study.

24. I don't know how to study.

25. I feel like my teachers hate me, so I can't be bothered doing any work for them.

26. I find it really difficult to get organized for school every day; I need help getting organized.

27. I really want the confidence to speak in public, but it terrifies me.

28. I made a mistake a few years ago, and now I'm labelled at school for it.

29. All this talk of interviews is freaking me out; I've no idea what to do in them.

30. I'm being bullied and it's making my life hell.

21 I just can't seem to focus at school.
22 I'm not getting good grades and my parents aren't happy about it.

I decided to look at these two chapters together because the same issue of focus pops up, and the consequences of that lack of focus or the "vicious cycle", as the student describes it, are obviously important, too. My main concern when I read this wasn't the student's lack of focus in school, but the student's belief that *I just can't do it*. I want to look at this statement in two different ways. We'll look at how to improve your focus in a few minutes, but for now, let's look at these "limitations" a little more because these are problematic.

⏸ Limiting Beliefs

Statements that begin with "I can't . . ." or statements such as "I'm not enough", or "I'm not . . ." are called Limiting Beliefs and they do exactly what they say on the tin: they limit us. In Chapter 10 you looked at your values and beliefs, and I highlighted that these need to be things that help you, things that allow you to grow in life. Limiting Beliefs don't allow for progression, they paralyze you, and anything that prevents progress from taking place needs to go, and needs to go now! None of us were born with these Limiting Beliefs; we've picked them up from somewhere along the way, maybe from something someone said to us or something we overheard. Now if you weren't born with these beliefs, and instead you found them somewhere and chose to keep them, that means there was choice involved, agreed? And if you had a choice in hanging on to them, then I think you'll agree that you also have a choice in getting rid of them or letting them go, agreed?

Let's use a metaphor and imagine these beliefs are like an item of clothing that no longer fits us or serves its purpose. Like our first school shirt we now can't get our arm into now or a rain jacket that's not actually waterproof. That's what

Limiting Beliefs are like: they don't fit us anymore, we've outgrown them, or they no longer serve their purpose.

STEP 1: Write down a Limiting Belief that you currently hold, remembering that this is something that you think you cannot do:

STEP 2: Write down how you THINK this belief helps you or how you THINK you benefit from having this belief:

Our mind can play tricks on us, and it doesn't always allow us to have rational thoughts, so it's important that we explore the reasons for hanging on to these Limiting Beliefs. For example, if I hold on to the Limiting Belief that I'm not good at meeting new people, I might think this helps me because it stops me from speaking to new people straight away and making a fool of myself. I mean, what if I say something stupid? I allow myself to think that this Limiting Belief protects me.

Here's another example: Let's say I believe that I'm not good at art. How does this help me? Well, it means I don't have to make an effort in art class, so I can goof around and chat to my friends. Or it means I've got an excuse for not getting good grades in the subject. Or what about this example: *I'm not good enough to go to university.* How does this help me? Well, here's another excuse that means I don't have to try hard, I don't have to make the choices about courses like other people, and I don't have to worry. Bingo! In a weird way, it's like our Limiting Beliefs are protecting us, or keeping us safe, but they don't really. Yes, most of them will attempt to keep you in your comfort zone, but how many successful people have stayed in their comfort zones and not dared to take a risk?

STEP 3: Realize that these are not facts, but beliefs, and not even helpful beliefs, but Limiting Beliefs. Do you agree? And do you agree that because they don't help you, we need to bin these beliefs? Yes?

▶ Then let's do it!

STEP 4: Create a stronger belief that helps you progress and achieve.

For the student who believed *I just can't seem to focus at school, so I get bad grades and complaints from Mum and Dad*, a more optimistic and helpful belief would be *I believe that I can overcome challenges in school*. Like a new item of clothing, you might want to try a few different beliefs on for size and then pick one that feels most comfortable. You might prefer the belief *I know I can focus at school when I put my mind to it*, or *Asking for help is a sign of strength, a sign that I want to do better*. They are your beliefs, so feel free to add some humor to them, and make sure you are comfortable with them. If we stick with the image of beliefs being an item of clothing, then keep in mind that as you grow, some items of clothing won't fit you as well, so you end up having to replace them with items that are comfortable to wear. The same is true with some beliefs we hold on to. Perhaps they no longer help you or perhaps you're no longer comfortable holding on to them.

Focus

How people focus nowadays, I have no idea! There's a wealth of distractions everywhere we turn; it's no wonder sometimes my audiobook has been playing for half an hour and all of a sudden I've no idea what's going on or what the topic is about.

⏸ How do we know when we are focused? Is focus something we can develop? How?

Have you ever watched a movie you were totally engrossed in, and when it came to explaining the plot to your friend, you could tell it word for word, with all the key details, plot twists and turns? But when it comes to explaining the last few pages of that chapter in your history book to your friend, you're lost. How does that happen? How did you focus on the movie for so long but not the written material?

You can tell you were focused on the movie by the way you can explain what you saw, felt, and heard in so much detail. Were you able to do that for the written material? Probably not! The reality is of course that we're usually more focused on things that matter to us. But we're also more likely to remember things we already have a bit of background knowledge on, too. It's as though we need something to link the new information to. Teaching someone about the consequences of the Russian Civil War might not go well if that person has no connection to Russia in the first place, let alone to the Civil War. However, if we helped that person create a foundation of knowledge on Russia, then they are more likely to be able to focus on the lesson and remember the new information as it will make more sense to them. One of my students was more into the role that people played in history rather than events themselves. She suddenly got very interested when I mentioned Serbia in one of lessons on the causes of World War I. Why? She was interested because her grandfather was Serbian, she was interested in learning about his life, and now she immediately had a link to help her remember some information she was not hugely engrossed in before. From then on, we did our best to create a personal link or a link which included people more so than events, and this helped her focus better. She had a connection.

Let's try an experiment. Read the following paragraph.

This summer my husband and I travelled to the US again; we've been there before and love it. New York City was our first stop. Man, I just love that place. Despite the hot and sticky summer heat of the city, we had a ball!
There's something amazing about the city, from Rockefeller Center to running through Central Park, I just love the atmosphere. We stayed at the Marriott Hotel near Times Square, which was a fantastic location with a great gym and magnificent city views. We had five nights there and then flew to Miami. Steve had been to Miami years ago; I've never been. I thought Dubai and NYC were hot, but I've never felt as hot as I did for those six days.
Apparently, they were having a heatwave! The highlight of Miami? Seeing Dwayne Johnson at the premiere of Ballers. *What a guy, and definitely a fantastic role model for young people.*

⏸ Okay, so here's a little experiment to test your focus just now on this part of my summer trip. If you had to relay to someone what you had just read, what did you notice?

⏸ What did you remember from the passage?

How did you remember those points? What made them stand out?

Did you remain focused for the entire passage? If so, how? What did you do to ensure you stayed with the story?

Did you zone out while reading it? Did you recognize you had zoned out? If so, at which point? Do you know what caused you to zone out?

I often find that if I zone out when reading something, it's because there's either something on my mind or it's because as I read the material, it reminds me of something else and my mind wanders down a different path. This is why I read with a pencil in hand, not just to underline things that are important to me, but to mark where I have lost focus, and I can then go back to it.

⏵ Can you learn to develop more focus?

Of course you can. If you zoned out while reading the passage about my trip to the US, try reading it again and this time immerse yourself more in the story. Create a picture in your head of what's going on, try to hear certain things, and feel what it would be like to live that experience. Or, can you link it to a similar experience you've had? These techniques will help to give you more focus because you're starting to build connections to it. If you were able to focus on the passage from the beginning, maybe it was because you connected it to a previous experience you had yourself. Or perhaps you zoned out also because of a previous experience you had that was related to the passage—you might have started wondering when you will visit New York City!

Training your mind to "come back" is like training any other muscle in your body. It takes time, and it takes practice. The best thing for you to begin doing is to notice and recognize when you've drifted off or zoned out and bring yourself back. This is one of the many benefits of mindfulness where you focus on the present. I've already recommended Headspace as a great introduction to mindfulness. Being mindful while listening to a guided audio just a few minutes a day will help you to become more aware of when you drift off, and it strengthens your ability to maintain focus.

Naturally, if there is something on your mind, then this is going to interrupt your focus. If we are anxious or stressed about something, then that takes up a lot of the mental energy we need to be able to focus. However, when we are more aware of what's going on in our heads, we develop our self-awareness. Do your best to notice when you feel anxiety creeping up on you. Being aware of it gives you power over it; it gives you the ability to control it before it controls you. Have a look at the chapters on stress and anxiety in Part 1 and use some of the techniques identified there to nip these unwanted feelings that are distracting you in the bud. Even if the techniques don't work the first time, keep going. Like everything, it takes practice. The more aware you are of your thoughts, feelings, and emotions, the more you will be able to manage them.

One of my close friends, a primary school teacher, told me something one of her very young pupils said to her one day. "Ms. Halpin, I don't think you understand, all these numbers and letters are this big", he said, holding his arms widely outstretched. "But my head, Ms. Halpin, it's only this big", he said as he brought his hands around his own head. "It doesn't fit in!" Believe me, all your knowledge will fit in, but not if your head is occupied with other things. When you learn to manage your own state of mind you'll have more room to focus.

▶ What can you do now?

Practice, practice, practice! Take any information at all and give yourself a few minutes to watch, read, or listen to it. Then explain it to someone else if possible or summarize it yourself. Draw an image if you like, whatever helps you. Notice any desire to zone out, or any actual zoning out, and then bring your attention back to the task. This is a skill, and as with any skill, it's not going to be come magically overnight. Think of it like becoming an endurance athlete, and do a short, simple task every day. Stretch and challenge yourself at the end of the week by increasing the time you spend reading, listening, or watching and notice your progress. It's like going to a mind gym! Bottom line? You CAN focus on school; you can focus on anything you want to.

KEY TAKEAWAYS FROM THIS CHAPTER:

❶

Your mind is a muscle, and like any other muscle in your body, it will get stronger the more you work it. Increase your level of focus gradually each day in different ways, training your mind to simply "come back" when you notice it has strayed.

❷

Contrary to popular belief, we generally don't multitask very well, especially when it comes to important things. Develop the habit of single-tasking to improve your focus; one thing at a time.

❸

Be aware of how you speak to yourself when it comes to your ability to do something. Your brain will follow the simple instructions you give it, so remember *I can focus easily for twenty minutes* is much more constructive than *I can't focus.*

"When you focus on problems, you get more of them. Guess what you get when you focus on solutions?"

LINDA BONNAR

23 I can't get motivated to study.

But I bet you can get motivated to do other things that you WANT to do, right? I worked with a young lady, let's call her Sophie, on exactly this topic. Let me share her story.

Sophie told me in a session that she really, really wanted to get more motivated to study. Her parents heard her say this time and time again, and still, nothing was happening. Weeks would go by, and still, the books hadn't been opened. Sound familiar to any of you?! In fact, her dad asked her straight out one day before we started a session, "If you're not studying up in your room, what are you doing?" and she replied simply, "My art, of course!" We used this as the starting point of our motivation session because Sophie had no problem getting motivated to paint, draw, or be creative, so it's not like she just had no motivation whatsoever. When Sophie and I spoke about her passion for art, she said she loved to create things; she loved making things look better and improving things. Her art projects allowed her to do that, whereas she didn't feel that studying did. Aha!

We all operate from a set of patterns, so the way you go about doing something that you feel motivated about, like Sophie and her art, can give you clues on how you could go about tackling projects where you have zero motivation. I asked Sophie about the steps she had taken before she began working on a piece of art and this is what she shared with me:

1. She cleans her workspace up because she knows she can't be very creative in a messy environment.
2. She sets up her easel and chair and makes sure it's in the right place in her room with the right light, depending on the time of day.
3. She organizes all her tools depending on what she's doing, so if she's painting, then she gets her paint ready, and checks all of her paint brushes.
4. If she's not painting something from her imagination, then she finds the image she wants to create and makes sure it's positioned correctly.
5. She gets her paper and then she's ready to paint.

Sophie explained that it might take her a few hours to complete a painting as she likes to take a break from it and come back to review it with a fresh mind. (This is going to come in very useful in a few minutes!) So how can we get Sophie motivated to study? Since creating and improving things is so important to Sophie, I asked her how she goes about creating and improving herself. What is she doing to create and improve her future? What is she currently doing to create the life she wants? What is she doing to ensure she can live the creative life that she wants? By investigating these types of questions, Sophie very quickly saw that by making greater efforts to study now, she is improving herself and her chances of going to the university she wants to. She frequently spoke about making other things better, but forgot about her own continuous personal growth. By highlighting to Sophie that she can fulfil these values of creativity and improve her grades, she saw things in a whole new light. But our job didn't finish there. Sophie admitted that she felt more motivated by this realization, but something still held her back, she just didn't see the point in studying. She saw the point of self-improvement and of being creative in many ways, but she didn't enjoy studying, and therefore wasn't interested in investing her time in it. She said, "There's just something so boring about the word 'study'. It implies work, and I don't like work!"

It's important to remember that the labels we put on things affect how we think and feel about those things, like "work". I asked Sophie to think of other names or labels she could put on the process of completing her school tasks and preparing herself for university, and after throwing out a few ideas, her face suddenly lit up when she said "Professional Development"! I found it surprising that a seventeen-year-old would use this expression because I associate it with a workplace environment. But here's a very good example of me putting MY ideas and MY beliefs or associations onto Sophie, and of course, that's not helpful. So, Professional Development it is! "It makes me sound like I'm doing important work, and I like that", she said.

Great. But our job still isn't done because Sophie said she hadn't developed the habit of studying. She actually didn't know where to begin, and this worried her a little. Here's the trick: because Sophie knows what she needs to do to get to work on her art, she can simply use the same procedure for her study. She'll make sure her desk is tidy, make sure the workspace isn't too bright or too dark, she'll organize the equipment she needs. If she needs her textbooks, then she'll place them near her, so she doesn't have to leave every two minutes to get a different book. If paper is the last thing Sophie gets before she paints, then why not let her exercise book or her lined paper be the last thing she gets before she begins her Professional Development?

"But I don't think I can study for hours on end or write my history paper in one straight go!" Sophie told me. "If it was a painting, what would you do?" I asked her. "Well, I would take breaks, then come back and review my work with a fresh mind. I find it helpful and straight away I notice things I can improve on in my work", Sophie told me, very matter-of-factly. I asked her, "Can you do that with this history paper?" to which she replied, "Of course I can. WOW, this is easier than I thought it was going to be!"

There we go! By understanding what was important to Sophie and then investigating the patterns she used to complete a task she loved, we were able to apply these values and strategies to another area of her life. We also found out that the very word or process of "studying" wasn't something Sophie liked or valued, so we changed it to something she did like and could see value in, which was Professional Development.

> ⏸ If you love being creative but don't necessarily love studying, then ask yourself how you can you be creative in your study.

What can you do to create more creativity while working?

What kind of ideas can you come up with?

Likewise, if the term "studying" de-motivates you, then give it another name. You're not changing the actual activity, but by changing the name you put on it, you change the way you feel about the activity, and this in itself can help increase your level of motivation.

KEY TAKEAWAYS FROM THIS CHAPTER:

❶

There are many reasons why we become de-motivated, such as when the task seems too big, there's a conflict in our values, fear, or when our goals lack clarity. You need to know what it is that's draining your motivation so you can get back on track.

❷

If the task seems too big, get your motivation back on track by breaking the task down into smaller bite-size chunks you can manage, then tackle them one at a time.

❸

If fear is holding you back, you've got to deal with it in order to move past it. Name your fear and write it down so it's out in the open. Then ask yourself, what are the chances of these fears really happening?

"If you really want to do something, you'll find a way. If you don't, you'll find an excuse."

— JIM ROHN

24 I don't know how to study!

As teachers, especially secondary school teachers, we often take it for granted that by the time students come into our classrooms, they know how to study, how to retain information, and then regurgitate it in an exam. But what if they don't?

Last year I did some history tutoring, and in my first chat with Jack, he said, "I just can't do history". Bonus points for you if you recognized the Limiting Belief of "I can't" in Jack's statement! He said he had no idea how to learn the material and it just never seemed to sink into his brain. Now, of course, Jack could use some of the methods we have learned to improve our focus in the earlier chapters so that he can create a personal link to people or places. But is that all studying is? Not really.

So, what is it and how do we do it? Well according to Dictionary.com, studying is "the application of the mind to the acquisition of knowledge, as by reading, investigation, or reflection". And again, how do I do it? Let's unpack the definition from dictionary.com definition for a moment.

1. Reading—just reading? I read all sorts of different things every day. But when I do, am I reading for enjoyment or reading to understand something? There's a huge difference between the two.
2. Investigating. Do I need to ask questions? What kind of questions? How can I find out more?
3. Reflection. How do I begin to reflect on the causes of World War I? How does this help me?

I don't think reading, investigating, and reflection are all there is to studying. What about watching videos? Or being involved in the process of making something? Is that a form of studying? Or would they come under the segment of investigation? In helping you to understand the word more and to know how to study, let's use the simple definition above, but let's dig a little deeper and maybe create some add-ons!

▶ Imagine you've got to study English poetry tonight. How do you even go about this?

1. **Reading:** Okay, firstly I encourage you to read with a purpose, not just reading for the sake of keeping your mum and dad happy. Ask yourself *What is the purpose of reading the poem for the first time? Could it be to get a picture of what it's about? Or to get a feel for it? Or to read it out loud to hear how it might sound to me? Could it be beneficial to read it three times to consider these three different viewpoints?* Absolutely! Then you might want to read it again to think about the images the poet creates, or to identify the similes and metaphors used, and so on. Read for a purpose, either to review, to clarify, or to find the answers to questions you have.

2. **Investigation:** Take on the role of a detective and dig a little deeper. How do detectives do their best work? By asking questions, of course! What questions do you have about what you've just read? Where could you find the answers? Could this lead you to read another poem? Reading some notes online? Or what about watching a short documentary on the poem itself? When you use other sources of learning, ask yourself *What's similar in the content and what's different? Have I learned something new from these other sources?*

3. **Reflection:** When you reflect on something, you think about what you've just read, or you consider someone else's perspective on the material. Was what you read commonplace at the time it was written? Why? Why not? Ask yourself *What are the key things that stand out for me here and how can I identify them?*

4. There are so many questions you could ask yourself, but for me, the key question to ask in order to study effectively is this one: *Could I now teach what I've just read to someone else?* If you can, even just a little bit, then you've been actively studying. You could also ask yourself the following:
   - If I was to paint a picture of what I just read, what would it look like?
   - If there was a two-minute podcast available on what I just read, how would it sound?
   - If I had to make a model to represent what I just read, what materials would I need?
   - If I had to label the poem with a feeling, what would that be?
   - If I had to write a tweet or text message about it, what would I write?
   - If there could only be one image to represent what I just read, what would that look like on Instagram? Or as a video on Snapchat?

⏸ Think about how you might read a long email or message from someone important to you. Would you just skim over it thinking you know what they meant? No, you'd probably take time and look at the details the person has included. Have they asked you questions you need to respond to? How will you make a note of or remember to answer these questions? Have they given you details like times or dates? How do you make these things stand out? The bottom line here is this: What methods do you use to remember things that are important to you?

People have different learning styles, just like we have different thinking styles. You've probably heard your teacher mentioning visual, kinesthetic, and auditory learners. We all have a preferred learning style, but that doesn't mean we can't learn any other way, it just means that one way seems to be stronger for us. Take visual learners, for example, who learn through seeing and watching. They tend to be very good at math or something like spelling. Think about how you learned to spell or count as a child. Chances are, if you used your fingers to count, or you tried to spell words by phonetically sounding them out, then things like addition and spelling might not be your strongest point today. People who learn to do math or spelling visually, by seeing the numbers and words written down, have a tendency to be better at these subjects.

Does this mean that if you want to be better at math and spelling that you only watch videos to enhance your study experience and improve your retention? Sadly, no! We don't want to focus on only using our strongest learning style, but instead use a combination of those learning styles. Watch, listen, and do as much as you can.

A student recently said to me that she found it really difficult to study history. In an attempt to help her, her history teacher had told her to write out notes and read over them, so she did. "Did this help?" I asked her. "A little, but not as much as I'd like. I just don't get the picture in my head from reading and writing", she replied. Bingo! This is an example of how people show you the best way they process information. In the answer above, the student told me that in order to process new information, they need, or prefer, to create a picture in their mind. She wants images because this is how she learns best. Reading and writing out her notes helps her a little, but what would happen if she was to watch actual videos about the historical people, places, and events she's studying? Probably a lot more!

And with a combination of watching, listening, reading, and writing, what's going to happen? You guessed it, a whole lot more! Create a combination of as many learning styles as you possibly can to reinforce the information you're studying, and you will be off to a great start.

⏩ Coaching hat off

Coaching hat off for a minute and teaching hat on here to quickly make a point about where you study. The old school idea says that you must have one area for study, a quiet space with all of your learning materials within easy reach. Now, that's great, especially if you have an area like that in your house. But what if you don't? Does that mean you may as well give up now because you don't have a designated study area? No way! In my own experience as an IB and A-Level teacher, students often tell me that because they are used to studying in one area of their home, they go blank when they go into the exam hall to sit their exams because the environment is unfamiliar and feels weird for them. My advice is to get used to studying anywhere and everywhere you can. Listen to podcasts as you get some exercise, watch some videos on a bus or train as you travel, or have a discussion with your friend about the material you've been revising. Don't limit your studying area to just one space, be open to learning in a variety of environments in a variety of ways, and you will enhance your learning experience.

As a teacher, I always encouraged my students to make flash cards or quiz cards that they could use with each other. They loved them and said they got a lot out of testing each other in small groups. They said that even just by reading out the question to the group they felt they were studying. You can also just test yourself using the flashcards—it's one of the strongest study techniques out there. Coaching hat still off, one of the best ways to check you've learned something is to teach it to someone else, and this in itself is a form of studying.

Remember:
1. Vary the location in which you study.
2. Vary the methods you use to study, and use all of your learning styles, not just one.
3. Quiz yourself.
4. Teach someone else.

⏸ Now is a good time to reflect on the definition we used from Dictionary.com, and while I'm not going to answer the question for you, I'd like you to think about what studying means to you now.

1. Do you now have a different understanding of what it means to study? If so, how?

2. What changes can you begin to make today to enhance the way you study?

3. From reading this chapter, what else do you think you might need to allow you to study more effectively?

KEY TAKEAWAYS FROM THIS CHAPTER:

❶

Studying is a skill, and like any other skill, there are lots of different things we can do to improve our ability to study more effectively. Studying is not one size fits all, so it's important to find out what works best for you individually. Be open to different strategies and techniques.

❷

Simplify your study notes, do not rewrite your entire textbook; think about bottom-lining pieces of text in your own words and coding information in different ways, e.g., circle key names of people, box keywords, and underline definitions.

❸

Create a story from the information you have read, and this will help you store it better. Stories help us connect and make sense of things, plus, your brain will naturally seek out a coherent structure for the story, too, making it easier to remember and recall the information when needed.

"The capacity to learn is a gift; the ability to learn is a skill; the willingness to learn is a choice."

BRIAN HERBERT

25 I feel like my teachers hate me, so I can't be bothered doing any work for them.

I've always been interested in how the relationship between a student and teacher can affect how motivated or how interested the student is. There could be a few things true about this chapter statement, but the first thing that springs to my mind is the thinking errors that have popped up. Can you spot them?

There's an element of mind-reading in there for sure, and then there's feeling versus fact. Before we go any further, let's make sure that we've acknowledged these thinking errors and named them so now we can work on dealing with them.

Firstly, feelings are not facts at all, and just because we feel something doesn't make it true. Secondly, we say we feel like things *are* a certain way, well, how do we know? Always check for evidence. In developing the skill of asking ourselves better questions, here's my question to anyone currently experiencing this particular issue: How do you know your teacher hates you?

Now I'm going to mind-read here for a few minutes and think about the things that might have popped up for you based on my experience, and the things that have been said to me, too.

- He/she gives me rubbish grades.
- They don't talk to me like they do to the other students.
- I always give the wrong answers.
- I'm not good at the subject.
- They never praise me.
- They speak to me differently.
- They've emailed my parents recently.

158 • PRESS PLAY

Can I tell you a quick story for a second to help shed some light on this subject? It was in Year 12 History one morning, a few years ago, and I was handing back essays that I had marked over the weekend. One student got his essay back and immediately I heard the rant take place with his peers about his grade. I turned around and asked him if everything was okay, and he said, "Miss, why do you hate me so much? Why can you just never give me 20/20? Why is it always 17/20? What have I done to you?" If you read, look, and listen to the words this student used, you'll notice how it's all very personal: *you, me, you, me, you.* The student has equated the number I placed on his work with how much I like him as a person. "Excuse me?" I asked. "It's true, Miss. Look at John's! He got 18/20. I mean, come on!"

As always, we have a choice in how we react to things. I didn't mind the first comment, but I disliked the second comment, which created a comparison between students, among other things. I made the best choice available to me with my skill set, and told the student, "Let's make one thing very clear here, Gary. I know how to separate my students from their work, and after years of practice, I'm very good at it. I mark work based on the historical skills that are displayed and nothing else. If you feel that marks are given for other purposes such as liking one student over another, then I think we need to have a separate conversation. Here's my suggestion, I do make mistakes in my marking sometimes because I'm only human, so how about you read through your essay again with your mark scheme, identify the areas where you feel you've been unfairly marked, and we'll have a conversation about it? If the work is deserving of a higher mark, then, of course, I'll award the historical skills and content displayed in the work. But I NEVER mark the person; I mark the work. Please consider that".

The class weren't sure how to respond, but it gave us all something to reflect on. A teacher marks the work they are presented with, and that's it, regardless of who the student is. An essay that achieves 10/20 does not mean the student is "bad" or bad at history; it means the writing produced simply hasn't met the marking criteria. If you think your teacher doesn't like you because of the grades your work is awarded, ask yourself if the work meets the criteria of the higher mark bands. If you think it does, and you feel you've been hard done by, then speak to your teacher in a calm and polite manner, avoid saying "you", and instead focus on creating a solution to move forward with. It could sound something like this:

"Miss, thanks for making my essay. I worked really hard on it and when I read over the mark scheme, I feel I've met some of the criteria in the higher band such as . . . Would you have time to look over it again with me, please?"

> I'm not here to say that all teachers are right in what they do and in what they say. We all make mistakes. I've made mistakes in things I've said to students before, and I've learned that it's wrong not to apologize just to save face in these incidents. If you find yourself saying a teacher speaks to you differently, then ask yourself, how do you speak to them? Do you show respect and manners? Do you participate? Do you give the impression you care and want to make an effort? Because I've been in that situation where I really, really wanted to give up on students before, in fact, I'm not ashamed to say that I have. Especially when repeated patterns of no books, no homework, not even a pencil case to a lesson in many cases, had happened one too many times. What message do you think that gives the teacher, and indeed your fellow students, in a classroom? Yup, not a very positive one. Reflect on your choice of words and your choice of behaviour first before you make assumptions.

If we look at the second part of the issue stated, *so I can't be bothered doing any work for them*, ask yourself how helpful this attitude is. The student has associated a feeling with a fact, they've done some mind-reading with no sign of any evidence and then developed a defensive attitude. *Well, you don't like me, so I don't like you.* It's not a very helpful way of thinking. Think about how this student's decision of choosing not to do any work is going to affect the student-teacher relationship now. Can you imagine the conversations that will take place at the next parent-teacher meetings? It is hardly a step towards a positive relationship, that's for sure!

What's a more constructive step this student can take to build a better relationship?

Unfortunately, I know we probably all know that *one* teacher who does have a chip on their shoulder, who is out to teach a student a lesson or to take their anger out on them. I'm not saying this doesn't happen, and I certainly don't want to ignore this side of the equation either. If you feel there is a level of unfairness taking place, then make sure that you speak to someone in school that you trust. But make sure you've made time to reflect on your choice of behaviour and maybe even speak to someone about that first, too. Thankfully, there is usually a method to your teacher's madness! They have your best interests at heart. If something is bothering you about a particular subject or teacher right now, then get it out of your head and onto paper right here:

Now do your very best to look at the positive intention behind your teacher's choice of behaviour for you. What could he/she really be trying to do for you?

Remember, it might even be helpful to put yourself in their shoes for this exercise or to ask a friend to help you with this. If you were that teacher, what would your positive intention be? We need to be realistic and ask ourselves if this positive intention could be true right now for your teacher, too.

You've got to do your best to make things easy for yourself at school because it can be tough enough both inside and outside of those walls. Ultimately, your teachers are there to educate you, not to be your best friend or your pal. If you feel there are inappropriate relationships taking place and you're concerned for yourself or a friend, it is imperative that you bring this to the attention of an appropriate member of staff at your school. Now go and do your homework!

KEY TAKEAWAYS FROM THIS CHAPTER:

❶

There are times when our emotions may not be telling the truth and are simply producing an emotional response within us, like feeling your teacher doesn't like you when it's the work they are criticizing and not you as a person. It's important to check the facts or we can end up saying and doing things based on what we assumed is happening, and not the actual situation.

❷

Step back and ask yourself better questions before you make accusations about someone or a situation: *Am I looking at the whole situation and not just one part? Am I choosing to listen to my feelings or considering the facts in this matter?*

❸

If you want to get different results, you need to do something differently. And you have the opportunity to do something different every minute of the day: you can choose a different attitude, a different tone, a more positive work ethic, ask for help—take control and create the change.

"Teachers open the door, but you must walk through it yourself."

CHINESE PROVERB

26 I find it really difficult to get organized for school every day; I need help getting organized.

Being organized is a wonderful habit which anyone can develop at any stage in their life. So, it doesn't mean that you can't get organized, it just means that you haven't been very organized up until now! First of all, ask yourself if this is an issue pertinent to school only, or across other areas of your life, too. Because if you can get yourself organized for other activities or events like camping or a soccer game, then you can get organized for school, too. If you do feel it's a habit that you notice across many/all areas of your life, then let's look at that.

> First, to get prepared and organized, you need to know what you are getting prepared and organized for. Let's imagine we're getting organized for school on Monday and we'll work backwards from there. If you don't have a schedule, then you need to make one.

STEP 1: Make a copy of your timetable in a way that it makes sense to you, remembering that different people learn and think in different ways. If you are a highly visual person, then you could think about pictures or symbols that represent the subjects. If you're a genius on a computer, then whip yourself up a great Word or Excel document, or if you prefer good old pen and paper, then choose that. You could make yourself a wall chart for your room and add Post-it notes to it whenever anything changes. Creating something that works best for you is often a process of trial and error, so give different methods a go. It's like throwing spaghetti at a wall: some of it will stick, and some of it will simply slide off!

STEP 2: Identify the specific books and pieces of equipment that you need for each period and add it to your list. Make the list as specific as YOU need it to be. It could look something like this:

	Monday	Items for lesson	✓	Tuesday	Items for lesson	✓
Period 1	History	Textbook Exercise book		Spanish	Textbook Exercise book Headphones	
Period 2	Math	Textbook Exercise book Math set		PE	Shorts, T-shirt, socks, trainers, shower gel, towel	

If you've got activities after school, then make sure they are identified on your schedule, too, because this isn't just about getting organized for your school day, but getting organized for life.

STEP 3: DO IT! Because you want to be more organized, you've got to make time to do it. How long will it take you to get organized? Realistically? A few minutes or maybe twenty minutes? Figure out what works for you.

What else do you need to be more organized now?

Most of the people I work with say that not having enough time prevents them from being as organized as they would like. And here's the thing about time: we don't get more of it, but we can do our best to make better use of the time we have. I know that I can spend ages scrolling through social media on my phone or looking through pictures aimlessly, but what's the purpose in doing that? If my purpose is simply to pass the time and relax, then perfect! Great job! However, if my purpose is to get myself organized for a meeting the following day, then I'm not doing a very good job, because it's highly unlikely my meeting involves anything from my Facebook feed or my lovely selection of profile pictures either. You get where I'm going with this. Time is precious and because so much of this work evolves by asking ourselves better questions, the next time you find yourself scrolling aimlessly through your social media, ask yourself the question, *What is my purpose in doing this?* Something you're going to need is a diary or planner of some sort. Does your school provide you with one or can you get one yourself? Could you make something electronic? I'm particularly fussy about diaries and planners because I know that it has to be something I will use—there's no point getting it otherwise.

The bottom line is figure out how long you realistically need to get yourself organized for each day and set that time aside the night before. How do you do this? People have different ways of remembering things, but I'm going to use my husband as an example for this one. Steve's a very busy guy. He's a physics teacher, a Head of Year, a rugby coach, he goes to the gym, he paddle-boards, he gives talks on astronomy, and sometimes he's got all of these activities happening in one working day. What does he do? He takes fifteen minutes the night before a busy day to work through each activity/job and put everything he needs at the front door so he is ready to go the next day. Sometimes it might take twenty minutes, as he will pack different bags for different activities, just like you might have a school bag and sports bag.

The difference between Steve and me is that I'll make written lists and Steve tends to do a combination of mental and written lists. Who remembers things more? Haha! Yes, me! Because writing things down gets it out of your head and onto paper, and when you make your list of things you need, then you're more likely to remember these things because it gets reinforced into your brain. BOOM! Ticking off things on a short list can be very empowering and rewarding as it gives you a great sense of achievement, whether it's a list of items for the school day, a list of things to pick up in the shop, or a list of Christmas cards to send.

As a teacher, one of the most common things I tended to hear was "Oh! I forgot my book because I thought it was Monday". If you happen to lose track of days or specific things you might have to bring into school, like a project book or something you're lending to a friend, how would *you* remember it? What could you do to ensure you'd remember it? Remember, people have different ways of doing things, so identify what works for you by trying a few things out.

⏸︎ Has anything worked particularly well before? If your current method isn't working very well, what else could you try?

Is there anything that prevents you from putting this method into place today/this evening to be more prepared for tomorrow?

If yes, what can you do to overcome this roadblock?

Is there anything else you would need to get this method going?

Who could you ask for some help with this?

Where could you get these items you need?

Below is an example of this questioning process.

Q: What do you need to do to remember things?
A: *Well, I write things in my school planner, but lately I've noticed I tend to use a notepad beside my laptop more. Actually, you know what, Post-its on my phone always help because my phone is always with me.*
Q: Is there anything that prevents you from using this Post-it method on your phone today/this evening?
A: *No, I don't think so. Oh, actually, I'm nearly out of Post-its! That's not going to be helpful.*
Q: How can you overcome this?
A: *Mum does her shopping on a Tuesday so I can ask her to pick me up some then. In the meantime, my English teacher is great at providing us with stationery when we need some in class, so I can ask her, too. I've got no excuses.*
Q: Is there anything else you'd need?

A: *No, I've got everything I need. I do need to make the time in the evening, though.*
Q: Who can you ask for help with this?
A: *I could ask Dad to remind me; he's super organized. Or I can ask my friend Laura to send me a message, she's great with this kind of stuff, too.*

I'm not asking you to make a list of things you want to do each and every day, as this can be quite stressful. What I am encouraging here is focus, self-management, and action steps. It's good to make the short list of items you need for school, but even better to make a habit of going through this list, because these items are not going to magically appear in your bag or beside the door as my husband's does!

KEY TAKEAWAYS FROM THIS CHAPTER:

❶

Your life as a student can be super busy and being organized will help make things go more smoothly for you. Organized people know the benefits of developing a good set of habits and a routine to help them get things done and meet any deadlines efficiently.

❷

Use one planner for everything so you know exactly what's going on and when. Make a note of your individual subject deadlines for essays, homework, coursework, etc. Add family and personal events. When you mark something into your diary, ask yourself when you need to begin taking action to meet that deadline and mark that in.

❸

Give everything a place and keep things in that place: have individual folders/files for your individual subjects; keep your pens, pencils, highlighters easily accessible when you're working so you're not wasting time looking for things. If you make notes in school on loose pages, make it part of your study routine to file these notes each evening.

"For every minute spent in organizing, an hour is earned."

BENJAMIN FRANKLIN

27 I really want the confidence to speak in public, but it terrifies me.

We've touched on the topic of confidence a little when we looked at self-esteem in Chapter 1, so we're going to use this chapter to look at more ways of developing self-confidence, which you can apply to public speaking or any other activity. To start, I want you to choose a situation or activity where you would like to be more confident. Let's press play on overcoming this challenge.

> A key part of confidence is competence. They go hand in hand. Competence is your ability to do something well. Confidence is your belief about your ability to do something well. Competence with confidence is a great thing; confidence without competence isn't as constructive! Here's an example: Imagine I have no idea how to ski (I'm not competent), but I have lots of confidence that I can do it brilliantly first time I hit the slopes. It's probably not going to go very well. You probably have an image in you head of me hurtling down a ski slope like in a cartoon! Now imagine I've been skiing for a few years. I know what to do on the slopes (competence) because I have the knowledge and practice, and I believe in my ability to ski well (confidence). This combination is much more helpful.

> Firstly, in order to check your level of competence, ask yourself *When it comes to this activity I want to be more confident in, do I know what to actually do? What does it entail? What kinds of actions does it involve?*

If we don't know what we need to do to be successful in the activity, then we need to gain more knowledge and more practice in it. How much will be enough? I have no idea; that all depends on you. When I was learning to horse-ride, I picked up the skill of rising trot really quickly, but learning to canter was a different ball game altogether. I had to learn what to do first and practice to get better at it.

Secondly, when we say we want to be more confident in X, what does that really mean? Confidence means different things to different people. What does it mean to you in this context?

Here's an example: *By being more confident as a public speaker, I mean that I want to be able to stand tall and present my arguments logically. I want to maintain eye contact with the audience while speaking clearly. I want to look confident and sound confident.*

Notice how in the example the student is focusing on what they want, not on what they don't want, which is really important, as we mentioned in Chapter 4 on goal setting earlier. Some people will say to me "I don't want to look scared" or "I don't want to be nervous". Instead, always start your objective with "I want".

Thirdly, on a scale of 1 to 10 (10 being the most confident ever), how confident are you doing this activity right now?

How confident would you like to be?

Okay, we know what we have to do, and we know how confident we want to be. What stops you from being this confident in your chosen activity?

When I ask this question, here are some of the most common answers I get:

1. I'm worried people will laugh at me.
2. I'm worried I'll make mistakes.
3. There's a voice in my head that tells me I can't do it.
4. Nothing is stopping me, only me. I know what I have to do, I just need to do it!

Remembering that we can only control the controllable, can we do anything about number 1? No, if people are going to laugh then that's their choice; some people will laugh at anything. Can we do anything about number 2? Accept that you will make mistakes and that's part of learning. You can prepare and do the best you can, that's all; everyone makes mistakes. Can we control number 3 and number 4? Yes, because those are things that happen inside us. Let's work on them now.

Controlling your self-talk or internal dialogue

Remember back in Chapter 2 where we looked at thinking errors? Well, this is very similar, except it's not just a thought, but it's self-talk. When it comes to being confident, self-talk is critical. You've got to work on turning that negative chatter in your head into supportive, encouraging talk. You've got to become your own cheerleader.

How do you do it?

As you become aware of when the negative self-talk begins, notice what exactly is being said:

What tone is the voice using?

The role of this voice is usually to protect you in some way. Logically speaking, if you don't get up on the stage and speak, no one can laugh at you. Similarly, you can't make any mistakes if you don't participate. However, while we know the voice is trying to protect us, we still want to be able to do these activities competently and confidently, so we have to quiet that voice and get up on the stage. I recommend we tell the voice to be quiet politely. Tell that voice you know it's trying to protect you, but on this occasion, you need more support because you're getting ready to get on stage and be amazing. This might sound a little unusual but it's something successful people all over the world do—they learn to control that inner chatter, they learn to tell that voice *I GOT THIS*, and that's what we need to do here.

Borrowing Confidence

This is similar to the "fake it until you make it" attitude and the Superman/Superwoman Pose we spoke about earlier in Chapters 1 and 12 where you actually act *as if* you have the self-confidence of someone you admire greatly, someone you think is super confident. It might be a good friend, someone in your year group, or a celebrity. You don't have to know them personally. Pay attention to how your chosen confident role model walks and moves, look at their hand gestures, what's their body posture like? (It's always going to be head up and shoulders back!) How do they speak? What about eye contact when they speak to others? What you're doing is modelling confidence from someone you believe to be confident.

Affirmations

Affirmations are positive statements said to support and encourage a positive mindset, positive thinking, and beliefs about ourselves. Two things to keep in mind when making affirmations is to use "I" statements. For example, I often tell myself *I am training my body to run longer, stronger, and faster with every training session I do.* Remember to check your body posture (stand tall, shoulders back, head up) as you state your affirmations. There's no point repeating positive words if your body posture doesn't support them. This is why it's good idea to say your affirmations while you're standing in front of a mirror so you can make sure you're standing up straight, with your head up and shoulders back. Keep your feet hip-distance apart—you can always adopt your Superman/Superwoman Pose and put your hands on your hips as you repeat your affirmations.

I have affirmations about myself as a coach, about my running (as you saw above), about my writing, my marriage, everything! An example of an affirmation about public speaking might be *I am a confident public speaker; I deliver strong, well-structured speeches, clearly and calmly for all to hear.* I know you can come up with better ones, so take a few minutes to think of five affirmations that you could use on a daily basis to support your self-confidence.

KEY TAKEAWAYS FROM THIS CHAPTER:

❶

Self-confidence is your belief in yourself and in your ability to do something well. It's an incredibly important and powerful belief to have, and the more you practice being confident, the easier it will get.

❷

Get an instant confidence booster by changing your posture: stand up tall with your shoulders back and your feet hip-width apart. Hold your head up high and smile!

❸

Remind yourself of all the times you have been successful and confident. Allow these memories to fill your mind, hold them, then step forward in this confident state.

"Confidence is not 'they will like me'. Confidence is 'I'll be fine if they don't'."

— CHRISTINA GRIMMIE

28) I made a mistake a few years ago, and now I'm labelled at school for it.

It's very unfortunate that not only do we continue to label people, but we often label them based on one event. Yes, we label people with positive attributes too like "kind" and "generous", but think for a minute about the kind of labels which either yourself or your friends have put on people recently. Thick, stupid, slow, loser, and the list goes on.

Can you change the labels you've been given? Honestly? This would involve changing how people, or even one person, views you. Easy? Perhaps. Guaranteed to work? Hell no! Because when you ask yourself if you have any control over what other people think, say or do, you know for a fact the answer is no. That's where you've unfortunately got to leave it, because no matter how hard you try to change what someone thinks of you, for someone else to change their beliefs, it's got to come from them. Whatever you did a few years ago or a few weeks ago, for some people, that's what they will hang on to because that's what they *want* to hang on to. People will hang on to these labels because, for them, they see some purpose in it. Remember that we're focusing on controlling the controllable throughout this book and learning to accept the things we cannot change. You cannot change how people think and feel about you. Keep in mind that the truth of it all is that what others think of you is none of your business, which is harsh, but true.

▶ What do you do?

First things first, remember that the label someone has chosen for you is NOT a reflection of you as a person. A key takeaway here is to learn to separate people from their behaviours. An example of this could be "Oh, he's so thick, he got an E in his math test". This kind of label puts the focus on the person not being smart because of a math result when the truth is this is not a true reflection of who the person is. Separate the behaviour from the person. I do recognize that this is not always an easy thing to do, but by becoming more aware of what a big impact these little changes in our language can make, you're less likely to label people yourself, now and in later life. Here's another example: My husband and I are travelling around America, and he locks the keys in the car. He spends hours beating himself up about it, saying "I'm so stupid", when in fact that one action or behaviour is not who he is. Fair enough, it's not the smartest thing he's done, but it certainly doesn't make him stupid at all. Separate the behaviour from the person.

> Next, put the focus all on you, because that's who you are guaranteed to be able to control, of course. You've got a choice. You can spend your time, and put your energy, into doing your best to change how people think about you, and try to convince them to see you in a different light, but how realistic is this? Surely, it's more realistic to focus on you and how you feel about your behaviour.

What is it about this label that bothers you?

What can you do about this?

One of the things about labels is that although we want to keep them for jars, they can often affect us by highlighting some truths or things we'd prefer not to admit to ourselves. I know this isn't always the case, as school gossip has a tendency to create some peculiar stories. Believe me, I've heard my share of them! But we also need to be realistic here. For example, if you are choosing to bully others at school and the label of "bully" is placed on you, it's because some people believe that if the behaviour is repeated enough that a person warrants that label. If you feel your behaviour is something that needs to change, have a go at answering the following questions.

> You've heard the rumors, and the names people have chosen to describe you, your actions, and the things they think you've done. Do you think there's any truth in it?

PART 3: SCHOOL • 175

If no, then go and take a break from all this work you've been doing. If yes, how? Where is that truth?

Are you interested in changing this behaviour?

If you answered yes to the above question, have a go at the following questions to highlight some changes you can make. If you answered no, then that's a very different conversation to be had.

How did this old behaviour help you?

How will changing this behaviour help you?

What's a better choice of behaviour to move forward with?

When and where could you begin to implement this behaviour?

How can you begin to implement this different behaviour?

How will you know when you've been successful in making this change?

Is there anything that stops you from making it now?

What can you do to overcome that challenge you've identified above?

Is there anyone you can ask for help?

I know that answering those questions in an honest way wasn't easy, so give yourself a big pat on the back for doing it, and for beginning to make the changes already. Now, knowing and accepting that you cannot change what others think or say about you, what *can* you do to make yourself feel better about all of this?

Sometimes we welcome labels as they make us stand out and they make us seem different, which some people like. And sometimes we feel that if we consider the label to be positive for us, then we have to carry out a certain type of behaviour to maintain that label. Think about the "sporty one" of your group, or the "funny one", "the one who doesn't care about their looks", and so on. What kind of things do they do to maintain their place in the group or their label?

When I announced to my group of friends that I was going to start running, I honestly didn't get a lot of support or encouragement. Instead, my announcement was met with disbelief and laughter. This caught me off guard to be honest, and when I questioned my friends as to what was so funny about my new endeavor, they replied, "But that's not your role in the group! You don't run; you're not the 'running one', your place is at the bar getting the drinks for everyone after our game". I thought about it and decided that I didn't like any of those labels anymore, and I thought, surely I can change my role in the group. I mean, it's not like it's for life, is it? And so I did. But instead of just talking about it, I knew I had to follow that up with action and new behaviours because actions speak louder than words. I looked at the behaviours and patterns that I used, and identified small changes I could make, like running on my own to see how I enjoyed it, joining a running club and signing up for short races to get me motivated. I covered my Facebook with info about all my new activities and yes, I got some laughs and smart comments from a few people like "Are you running to a sale, Linda?" However, the more consistent I became with my new behaviour, the more accepting it was for me to have this new role or this new persona. I'm now known as "the crazy ultra-marathon runner one" or "the entrepreneur". Will it be this way forever? Probably not, but who knows, maybe I'll change it to "crazy horse lady" soon! Create the labels YOU WANT for YOURSELF in YOUR life and make sure your behaviour is consistent with your goals.

KEY TAKEAWAYS FROM THIS CHAPTER:

❶

At any point you can choose to play a different role in this story of life: you can choose to play the victim, the survivor, or you can choose to be the person who conquered those who tried to label you. The choice is always yours.

❷

Actions speak louder than words; if you'd like people to begin to see you differently, you need to choose different behaviours.

❸

People will see what they want to see themselves; that's about them and not you. Accept that just because you've moved on doesn't mean others have to, too.

"It ain't what they call you, it's what you answer to."

— W.C. FIELDS

29 All this talk of interviews is freaking me out; I've no idea what to do in them.

Getting nervous about interviews is perfectly natural. I know adults who get nervous about them, too. In fact, I remember waking up in the middle of the night to be sick before an interview once; it happens. While being a bit nervous is fine and it gets your adrenaline going, you don't want to be "freaking out", so the best thing you can do is to get prepared. I've put together five steps below which will help you calm those nerves and get interview ready.

Do your homework

It doesn't matter if it's a university place you're interviewing for, an internship, or even a part-time job at a local restaurant, do your homework and find out about the place you could be spending a lot of time at. Your interviewer will probably ask you why you want to go to that university/why you want an internship with that company or why you want that part-time job, so know something about the place you're applying to. What is it about it that appeals to you? Has the organization been in the media for anything that interests you recently? Doing a little bit of research can make a big difference. Do a Google search, and have a look at respective social media platforms, too.

Practice questions

Along with doing your research on the organization you're hoping to join, working on some practice interview questions is very helpful. Make a list of questions, write out answers to them, and have a friend take you through some mock interviews too. Typical interview questions will depend on the organization you're looking to join, but be prepared for the usual ones, such as:

Why do you want to join/work with this organization?

What are some of your strengths?

What will you bring to the organization?

What's one of the biggest challenges you've faced in your life so far and how did you overcome it?

Build rapport with the person

Remember that we like people who are like ourselves and building rapport with your interviewer or your interviewing panel is a really useful skill that can greatly improve your chances. One of the ways you can do this is to "mirror" the questioning words or phrases your interviewer asks. Use the words in the questions as "sentence starters" to get you off on the right foot. Here are a few quick examples to help you:

Q: *How do you **feel** about the current situation regarding X?*
The person wants to know how you feel about X, so make sure that you describe how you feel in your answer. Do you feel it's an injustice? Do you feel it's been well handled?
Example: *I feel the situation has greatly improved recently and things are really turning around now for the better.*

Q: *How does that **sound** to you?*
When asked how something sounds, tell the person how it sounds to you. Does it sound fair or unfair? Does it sound positive or negative?
Example: *That sounds great, and the points you've made have really resonated with me, thank you.*

Q: *Where do you **see** yourself in ten years?*

If you're asked anything about where you see yourself, create an image for your interviewer.

Example: *I have a very clear and focused vision for my future in finance. In ten years' time, I see myself...*

Illustrate your skill set

Your interview is your chance to shine and show your interviewer what you can really do. Before you start showing your interviewer how fantastic you are, make sure you have read and understood the required skill set for the job—don't just presume that every workplace/university course wants the same thing. Once you've done that, prepare examples to show your interviewer how you've used these skills or characteristics. Perhaps you've got incredible IT or people skills? Brilliant, give specific examples of how you've used these skills effectively. Perhaps you were faced with a challenge or problem and by using your effective communication skills, you were able to resolve the issue, which has since then resulted in your team having a more productive week. Don't just list your skills. Instead of saying "I'm great at languages", give evidence. Perhaps you have spent a summer in France and decided to stretch yourself beyond your school syllabus by reading French novels and listening to local radio shows while you were there.

Relax, you got this!

Perhaps you've already been practicing some of the relaxing or confidence-building techniques given in this book. Don't worry if you haven't, as I've got a few quick hacks for you here, too.

If you're nervous before your interview, or even as you prepare for it, remember to breathe slowly and deeply. Not only does this relax you, but as you slow down your breathing, you also slow down your thoughts, allowing you to regain your composure and answer the questions confidently.

Having a short mantra or phrase as you breathe can also be really useful. Sometimes I use something like *Inhale confidence, exhale doubt* or *I've got this* as I literally imagine exhaling any doubt I have about the situation. Try a few different phrases out. Whatever you choose, make sure that it suits you.

KEY TAKEAWAYS FROM THIS CHAPTER:

❶

Interviews are simply ways for people to find the right person for a position available. By making time to research the company, practice popular questions, and think about your own personal strengths, you're already in a much stronger position for the interview.

❷

Interviewers want to see how you can add value to the company so instead of listing what you know. Explain where you've applied the skill set you've gained and the solutions you've created.

❸

See the interview as a positive experience, an opportunity to learn, or to create new relationships, and you'll immediately reduce any negative feelings you may have about it.

"Talent will get you in the door, but character will keep you in the room."

— UNKNOWN

30 I'm being bullied and it's making my life hell.

If there's one thing I've never tolerated as a teacher, it's bullying. Bullying is repeated, deliberate or intentional verbal, physical, social, or cyber harm towards someone or a group of people. Bullying is not a one-off; it's not about catching someone on a "bad day". It's deliberate and it's repeated, it is a chosen form of behaviour.

Bullying can make your life hell. And it's not just confined to the school day nowadays thanks to the power of social media and the many devices we clutch. I've heard the stories. I've read about a fifty-two-page report on a WhatsApp group chat set up to slate other students. And I've lived the nightmare to the point where I even began questioning myself as a person because I started to think maybe there was some truth to what these people are saying to me. That's the thing about bullying that many people forget or choose not to consider: it's not that easy to "just ignore them" or "kill them with kindness" or "just forget about them" when it's happening every single day. And if you can ignore the bullies, then I have the upmost respect for you, because you're a lot stronger than I was.

▶ The first thing that you have to do is tell someone. I know it's cliché, and I am using the word I hate, but you *must* tell someone. Far too many people who are bullied don't tell anyone because they are worried it will make things worse, but while we have no evidence to prove that it is guaranteed to make the situation worse, I can sure as hell guarantee you that NOT talking about it WILL make it worse.

By not talking about it, we keep it hidden, and when we keep things like this hidden then it allows things like guilt and shame to grow; it's like we're blaming ourselves for it. Bullies thrive on that—in fact, anyone who is seeking that kind of power over someone else relies on their target not to tell anyone about it. By speaking to someone about it, you remove part of the power the bully holds over you immediately. Speak to someone, whether it's a parent, a teacher you trust, a friend, a family friend, a school counsellor, or even phone a local helpline if you're lucky enough to have such a service in your area. I know this isn't as easy as just blurting it out, so decide when you are going to do it, and reward yourself for when you do.

If you choose to speak to someone about it and things don't change OR if you're adamant about not going to speak to someone about it, then you've got to look at other options. One of these options could be that you work hard to change the way you view these people and their behaviour. You know from Part 1 that every behaviour has a positive intention, and yes, as odd as this may seem, this also includes bullying. Obviously, this applies to the bully and not the person being bullied. The bully gets something from their continuous deliberate exclusion, verbal slurs, or physical violence towards others. According to StompOutBullying.org, "A common reason that a person is a bully is that he/she lacks attention from a parent at home and lashes out at others for attention. This can include neglected children, children of divorced parents, or children with parents under the regular influence of drugs/alcohol". I think a student I worked with a few years ago put it best for me when they said, "But Miss, surely you've got to feel sorry for these kids who do these things. They are clearly lashing out at something wrong in their lives". True, true. A very mature way of looking at the situation for sure, but not always so easy to actually implement when you're in that situation.

Here's something to try out—imagine the bullies are wearing shirts/T-shirts with a particular slogan on them and that's what you see when you look at them. It can be a slogan of your choice, like *Please feel sorry for me* or *I bully because I was bullied* or *I call you names to feel better about myself*, but it needs to be a helpful one, not one that reduces you to their low standards of bullying. You could imagine them walking around in clown suits or in jungle outfits, something so completely alien and ridiculous to what they usually wear. Change how you view these people, and you begin to take even more control of the situation. Your brain is a very powerful tool and it's capable of incredible things, especially when you're looking for solutions or ways out of a challenging situation.

▶ If you are being bullied, then you need to make sure that you keep your head in a very clear space. By that, I mean, you *must* (I know, that word again, but it's an order here!) not allow the words used by bullies to gain any recognition whatsoever. Instead, let them brush right over you like a breeze. Yes, this takes mental strength, but you've got it within you. Find a positive statement that YOU like, and use it. Have it on hand whenever you have to be in the same room as these people or whenever they throw one of their comments at you. Smile to yourself, get that Superman/Superwoman Pose going, and say your statement to yourself. Make this your new habit. Keep in mind that your bullies want to get a reaction from you, they want to know that they are affecting you. When you choose to react in a different way it throws them right off.

▶▶ You could choose to interact with these people, too, and by that I don't mean start pushing them around, sending abusive messages, or shouting comments, but having a comment on hand which you use. If someone comments on your appearance (no matter how nasty), you could reply with, "Thank you, it's lovely to be seen/noticed". I know this might not come as an easy retaliation, but the fact is, someone who chooses this type of a reaction is not bowing to these people at all; they are showing strength. They have realized enough is enough and they've chosen a different route. I know a girl who said she used to make sure she replied with "I" statements when she was bullied in a previous school for the color of her skin. She used to reply with comments like "I really don't see it that way" or "You can say whatever you want, but I choose not to allow those words to sink in". My personal favorite reply that this lady shared with me was "You can say what you like, but Jada Pinkett Smith and Tyra Banks are laughing all the way to the bank".

Whatever you choose to do, remember that we all have a breaking point. We get to a stage where enough is enough, and that's when it becomes imperative that you tell someone about it. Never feel that you have to do this alone. StompOutBullying.org tells us that one in four students are bullied, and that's an incredibly high figure that simply must be stopped. The website also tells us that 8 percent of students miss one day of school a month due to bullying.

Bullying is something I can, unfortunately, relate to. One girl, who coincidentally was my best friend for years, decided to make my life at school a living nightmare. When I walked past her, she would shout things out, and would always make sure she was heard making these comments about me in front of other girls I was friendly with, who incidentally didn't speak to me when she was around. It got to the stage where I started skipping classes we were in together, which was a lot of my school day! When I did go to the classes, I would keep my head down, and not make eye contact with anyone. Because I had been such a chatty student before this, it didn't take long before my teachers saw the change in me and began to ask if everything was okay. I used to just nod and smile and say there were things going on at home when there weren't. I just thought it sounded so stupid and petty to say that my once best friend had turned completely against me and was turning others against me too.

I made up a story to my mum that I wanted to study law so I could move from business studies to history. The school said fine, they didn't seem to care anyways, and I joined history. In the classes where I wasn't with her I was an entirely different student, so when it came to parents' evening and some teachers said I was like a mouse and others said I was so chatty and bubbly, my mum just couldn't understand it. I eventually told her what was going on, and she said I was stronger than that other girl and that I'd be fine. She told me I couldn't miss out on classes because of one girl. She had no idea what it was like, though. It got to the stage where when my mum was at home during the day, I would phone her and pretend to be sick so she'd come and pick me up from school. But when she was working during the day, and both her and my dad had left the house for work early, I wouldn't bother going to school. Instead, I'd just get a lift into town in my school uniform in the afternoon, ready for her to pick me up on her way home from work. I thought I would become good at keeping the lies going, but I was an absolute wreck inside.

My life felt unbearable. I spent more and more time hiding at the stables and while I was desperate for the people there to see how unhappy I was, I also didn't feel able to talk about it.

I ended up leaving school in the January of my fifth year, when I was fifteen, and taking a year out. When I think about it now, I'm not really sure how my parents agreed to it, but I know I had reached my breaking point, and after the Christmas holidays, I was refusing to go back. But things began to fall into place for me, and after a few odd jobs here and there, I ended up getting a job at a riding school in Kildare, the Irish home of the horses. All of a sudden, I felt like I was living the dream. I was paid to ride people's horses, I made a fantastic group of friends, I had new doors in the equestrian world opened for me, and I just loved the environment I was in. I was thriving! My riding improved, my self-confidence improved, and I felt like I really belonged. There was no-one in the yard I avoided, I got along with everyone, and I used to spend my evenings chatting to the owners of the horses when they came to ride after their own working day. I loved it. As I gained this new confidence in myself, I started going out more when I travelled home for the weekends, and I actually began to enjoy socializing and meeting new people. The fear of seeing this girl was no longer there at all.

After a few months of working at the riding school, at sixteen, I knew I still had to go back to school at some stage. And I did. I moved schools, which was not easy to do in a small town in Ireland, but what a difference it made!

A few years later I was out with my friends in my hometown when I bumped into one of the girls who chose to bully me when I was in school. She apologized to me and said she had no idea the effect it could have on people. That same night I saw my bullies' ringleader, who had an entirely different approach, giving me the dirtiest looks ever, even mumbling horrible comments to me as I walked past her. It was proper childish playground material! I literally laughed out loud as I walk past her with my head held high, my Superwoman Pose on, and a smile all over my face.

Bullying is never acceptable and it can reduce a person to a shadow of themselves. You must speak up about it, and you must know that you are so much stronger than a person who chooses to bully you will ever be.

KEY TAKEAWAYS FROM THIS CHAPTER:

❶

Bullying can take many different forms, but it's always deliberate and consistent behaviour, not a one-off event. People choose to bully others because of negative factors in their own lives. It's nothing to do with you; you are the mentally strong person, not the bully.

❷

If you are experiencing bullying, you must tell someone you trust about it. Keeping quiet will never solve the problem.

❸

Remember having choice gives you power, and you always have a choice in how you handle a bullying situation: avoid the bullies where possible, or if you want to speak back, use assertive simple statements like "Get away from me". Never respond with violence or nasty remarks.

"People who repeatedly attack your confidence and self-esteem are quite aware of your potential, even if you are not."

—WAYNE GERARD TROTMAN

Family

The Challenges Dealt With In PART 4

31. There's loads of pressure on me to study something I'm just not interested in.

32. There are never conversations; it's always confrontations.

33. It's those same twenty questions when I get in the car every day.

34. I feel like I'm compared to my siblings all the time and I hate it.

35. I'm leaving for university next year, but my parents still treat me like I'm twelve.

36. My parents don't allow me to go out and all my friends are allowed out.

37. My parents keep asking me what I'm going to do after school and I have no idea.

38. I feel like I'm not being true to myself or true to my family, and it eats me up inside.

continued . . .

39. I'm fed up living away from my real home. We get shipped around a lot with my parents' work.

40. I'm worried my parents are going to get divorced.

31 There's loads of pressure on me to study something I'm just not interested in.

As a teacher, the amount of times I have something like the statement above is ridiculous! Mostly it was about studying medicine, especially if there were already doctors in the family. The young student would say that Dad is a doctor, Granddad was a doctor, and now they're expected to carry on the tradition. This is really hard if being a doctor is your family's dream, but not yours.

I recently spoke to another young lady who said her dad is pressuring her to join the armed forces in the UK. When she asked him why, he replied, "Well, I always wanted to, but I never had the chance to, and I know it will help you". Interesting! There are a few things going on here that I want to unpack with you. Firstly, let's take it for granted that what your parents want you to do with your life comes from a place of love and concern. We can often mistake it as a desire to control us, and believe me, with the way it is sometimes communicated to young people, it's easy to see why you would think that. But for now, we're wearing the belief that their wishes for you come from care and a desire to see you do well in life.

Parents sometimes believe that particular jobs or roles have the ability to make their sons and daughters happy. They might say things like, "Well, look at your cousin, he loves it", or "There's great money in it", or "You can help so many people", whatever it is. Do you see what's happening here? Parents have certain beliefs and values about particular jobs. We don't need to know why they have these beliefs at this stage but simply understand that they see their beliefs and values as being important and so try to get others, including you, to wear them, too. Not just try them on, but *wear* them. And of course, you know from reading the previous chapters that this simply doesn't work. You can see this in the example above of the dad who believes the army will be good for his daughter. In his mind, it will provide her with certain things, including an opportunity he never had. Yes, we can often confuse this with, *Oh, he just wants me to be like him, but I'm not,* but again, when we hold the belief that his statements come from a place of love and concern, then that puts a whole new light on it.

Could it be that this dad sees the army as a place that's good for a young girl to go, where she can learn self-defense and life skills, and where she can be considered on an equal footing to a male counterpart? See, this is a very different way to look at this than the thought *Just because he didn't get to go, he wants me to.* Remember, part of this work is about reframing. It's about taking the picture or image you have in your mind of a particular situation and creating a new way of looking at it, a new frame around the same situation.

And then, of course, there are parents who believe that they know what is right for you, and yes, quite often they do, but also sometimes they don't. There are parents who like to "keep up with the Joneses" and want to be able to say their son or daughter is studying X at Y university. Unfortunately, when people have that particular mindset, it's very hard to change it.

▶ So, what do you do?

Okay, before you go racing down your parents' throats with an assertive speech, do me a favor and think about what was said in the section above. Put yourself in your parents' shoes for a minute, really take on their role, their feelings, and most importantly, that place of care and concern for you, their child. If you're having trouble doing this, then take yourself to an objective area in the house, or outside if you have a garden. Having a friend to do this with will make it easier too, as they can ask you some questions. The point of doing this exercise is to remove yourself from a subjective area in your house, like your room, to help you gain a new perspective. Use something as simple as two bits of paper that represent you and your parents. Label the bits of paper if you like. Stand on your own marker and think about the message you want to give your parents. Think about where that message comes from. Why is it important this message is heard? You might even want to write it down:

Then stand on the marker that represents your parents. Choose one of them and really immerse yourself in that role. Stand like your parent, think about their mannerisms, their accent, and so on. Now think about the message you as your parent want to give, in other words, what would be the message your parents would want to give you? Where does this come from? What's important about this message?

You can write this down, too:

What do you notice when you do this?

Can you understand where your parents might be coming from?

What could your parents' positive intention be?

Remember we're not mind readers, but in this activity, we are learning to accept that their desire for our success comes from a caring place. Once you keep that in mind, you're ready to jump down their throats—NOT! There'll be no attacking anyone, but there will be conversations. Let's do it.

▶ Having the conversation

Having the conversation is always better than a confrontation, believe me. But I'm not saying it's the easy choice. I'm going to generalize here, but usually parents in this situation believe that they know best and that they are being helpful in trying to guide you as best as they possibly can. Perhaps they see something in you that you don't see in yourself? Perhaps the way they push you towards a particular career is because they see a certain talent in you. Could this be the case? Here's how you can go about having the conversation:

1. Ask your parents if you can have a conversation with them. YOU suggest the time and date, and even the place. Perhaps it could be an objective area, just like the exercise above, so there's no "territory" involved.

2. I understand that this can be a bit nerve-racking, so make a plan of what you are going to say.
3. Whatever you say needs to show you're taking responsibility for yourself, so focus on using "I" statements like "I feel", "I would like", "I appreciate", because you know that using "you" statements like "You make me feel" or "You never" places blame on someone and that's not our objective.
4. In your plan, make it known that you appreciate their continued support and you know their concern comes from a caring place. If you don't already know, then ask your parents what's important to them about you studying this career in particular. Asking your parents this question shows that you respect their values, too. Is it about stability and security? Family tradition? Financial security?
5. Before you begin campaigning to convince them to agree with your point of view, ask your parents to listen to what you have to say.

It could go something like this:

I value your continued support, and this morning I just want two minutes to be heard. I know that you would love me to go to uni to study medicine because you care about me, and you believe that a career in medicine is stable and will provide me with security for later life.

Note, this is all positive so far, and the use of "you" is okay here because it's not accusatory, you're simply acknowledging your parents' values.

I've thought a lot about my future recently, and I've spoken to Mrs. X at school, and I've had some career counselling on it.

Again, this shows you also value your parents' value of you having security for your future, and shows you have done your research.

We both know some of my strengths are in working with others.

Saying "we" shows your parents have been heard too.

And while I see the value in a career in medicine, it's not for me. I'm very passionate about education, and that's what I want to study at university. I value your love and support and know you'll support me in this decision.

And ideally any frustration ends there, and everyone walks away to live happily ever after, especially with a career in teaching!

⏩ What do I do if nothing changes even after I've had the conversation?

Okay, so this one is tough. You will need all of the above and more. If you've already had the conversation above and nothing has changed—in other words, your parents are still set you on studying a particular course—then it's time to ask for support. You are not expected to do this alone, and it's really important to know that. Make sure that you are doing your very best to understand where your parents are coming from, and even if you can't understand their exact reasons, then at least acknowledge them. At this stage, you need to make sure that your message is being heard, too. Remember, it's not about winning, or getting one up on your parents by making them change their minds, it's about being heard. I fully understand that this isn't easy at all, but what's the alternative? Go through with someone else's life plan for you so that you can have a "quiet" life? Remember that you always have a choice.

⏩ Where do I get this support?

This book is all about being resourceful and taking action, so I want you to think of people you know right now who might be able to help you out, and in what capacity. For example, is there an older sibling who can join a meeting with you or a close family member who understands what you might be going through?

Are there places which can support you, such as your school?

KEY TAKEAWAYS FROM THIS CHAPTER:

❶

Having difficult conversations can be tricky, so one of the best things you can do is to plan things out first. Get very clear on the objective of having the conversation and the meaning you want to deliver to your parents. Keep in mind that it's not about winning or getting one up on your parents.

❷

Be as prepared as you possibly can for any questions or points your parents might raise. This will show them that you are serious about your future, and in turn will encourage them to take your argument more seriously, too.

❸

Make sure that you understand what your parents have said before you respond to them. In these situations it's important that everyone is heard and understood or else more confusion is create. Ask for clarification if you need it.

"Pressure can burst a pipe or pressure can make a diamond."

— ROBERT HORRY

32 There are never conversations; it's always confrontations.

This issue popped up in a Skype conversation I had with a fantastic young lady recently, let's call her Jane, and it ties in with the previous issue. I'm going to use parts of the actual conversation I had with Jane to help you see things from a different perspective, as I feel many young people face the same kind of issue with their parents. I also want to show you how powerful some simple questions can be, too. If this issue is something you're currently facing, have a go at answering the questions I asked Jane in the spaces provided below.

In my conversation with Jane, she explained that she had given up on her dad. She felt that he was always against her and never supported her. She said she felt like he was always trying to control her, and she just wanted to be able to have a normal conversation with him instead of an argument. As a result, she had started avoiding him at home in the evenings and admitted that she didn't want to be in the same room as him for fear of getting the "twenty questions" every day.

I asked Jane, and I'm asking you now, too, to think of a recent time you had a conversation with the parent in question. Now, it's rare that a conversation will start out as a confrontation, it's almost as though it gets switched somewhere along the way, right? Unless you're in big trouble with your parents, and in that case, they've probably got a right to be confronting you. Jane said she believed the conversation turned into a confrontation as soon as her dad asked her, "So, have you made a decision about college yet?"

Now, for the conversation you're thinking of with your own parents, identify the point at which YOU think it changes:

The conversation continued.

Me: What makes you say it's at that point that the conversation changes?
Jane: Because it's a question and he always has to ask me questions because he wants to know everything I do.

PART 4: FAMILY • 199

Now imagine I am asking you the same question. In your conversations with your parents, where do they turn into confrontations?

Me: Could there be another reason for him asking you this question about your future?

Jane: No, he's trying to control me.

Now imagine I am asking you the same question. Could there be another reason for your parents asking you questions or making the comments they do?

Then the conversation then took a different kind of turn.

Me: I ask you lots of questions. Do you think I'm trying to control you?
Jane: No, I know you're trying to help me.
Me: How do you know?
Jane: Because your questions get me to move on.
Me: Could your dad's questions have the same purpose of getting you to move on? To encourage you to think about your future?
Jane: I guess so, maybe, but I feel like he's trying to control me with all the questions and when he says he wants to know everything I do at college. I don't want to have to tell him everything. It's like he's spying on me.
Me: And apart from the fact that your dad is clearly a spy, Jane [sarcasm!], could there be another reason why he asks you these questions?
Jane: I don't know!
Me: I bet you do.
Jane: Well, maybe it's because he cares, right? People ask questions about things they care about, like you.

In this instance, what would be your answer? Could your parent's questions or comments have a different purpose to the one you're thinking of?

What could this mean?

And then Jane's next comment was a kind of lightbulb moment for her.

Jane: Do you think he's worried about my future? He's got no reason to be; I know what I want to do. But he's my dad and I know he cares about me, and perhaps he is worried, too . . . It's not like I tell him much, is it?

In those few moments, Jane went from giving her dad the labels of "nosey" and "controlling" to "caring" and "worried". In coaching, we call this reframing, which means you put a different frame around something, so you see it differently. It's very powerful. Now, let's look at Jane's last statement again. It's powerful because she seems to know what she wants to do. Hence, she doesn't see the point in her dad questioning her. *But* does her dad know she knows what she wants to do after school? Do your parents know your plans?

Me: That's great that you know what you want to do. Have you told your dad your plans?
Jane: No! He won't support me.
Me: How do you know?
Jane: Because two years ago when I first told him I wanted to study acting, he laughed at me. That's not supporting me. I was mad. I was so mad at him. I still want to study acting.
Me: Do you know for a fact he was laughing at your choice for the future?
Jane: No, no, I don't.
Me: So how did you reply to this question the last time he asked you?
Jane: I shouted at him. I was so angry, I shouted, "Stop trying to control me!"

Okay! At this stage, the alarm bells started going off in my head and I took Jane through the conversation so far.

Me: So, let me get this right. Your dad walks into the kitchen and asks you a question about your decision for college, and you reply with "Stop trying to control me!" in an angry manner, right?
Jane: Yup, that sounds right! [She starts laughing]
Me: What's so funny?

Jane: Well I've just noticed that it was actually *my* response that caused the conversation to change, not Dad's question.

Me: Okay. Great, good work! Have there been other times when this has happened?

Jane: Yes. Sometimes I just don't want to talk about stuff with him, you know?

Me: I know. But does he know that?

Jane: I don't think he knows, but you keep saying parents are not mind readers and I need to remember that. Guess I need to talk a little more and maybe he'll ask me less.

Me: How would you know if this would work?

Jane: I'll have to try it, Linda, won't I?

Me: Great, when are you going to try it?

Jane: When I see him this evening, I'll do my best to think about better responses or even just having a chat with him.

> You cannot control what your parents say to you, but a conversation is a two-way process, and you play a role in that process. Think about the message that you're giving to your parents. The bottom line is they care, and they worry. They're your parents, that's what they do! I have no idea what it's like to be a parent, and I'd never pretend to, but I do know what it's like to attempt to communicate with people and build relationships with them, including teenagers. I used to be one too, a horrible one! So, trust me when I say that your silence doesn't produce more silence with your parents; it will often just produce more questions. Communicate with them as openly and honestly as you can.

Jane makes more of an effort with her dad now and has learned to look at things from his perspective. I've encouraged her, and many other young people, to use the "marker" exercise to help with this. Put yourself in their shoes more and ask yourself what it feels like. How do things look? What do you notice? Because things can look very different depending on where you look from.

KEY TAKEAWAYS FROM THIS CHAPTER:

❶

Communication is a two-way street, and the only person you can control in a conversation is yourself: your words, your tone, your body language. If you don't like the way the conversation is going, do something about it.

❷

Take a minute to view the situation from someone else's position, step into their shoes, and do your best to see what they could be seeing and feel what they could be feeling.

❸

In the conversation use specific examples where you can to support the point you are making. Using phrases like "You always" or "You never" not only overgeneralizes, but also points the finger of blame at the other person, which shows a lack of responsibility on your behalf.

> *"The biggest communication problem is that we do not listen to understand; we listen to reply."*
>
> — STEPHEN R. COVEY

33 It's those same twenty questions when I get in the car every day.

A few years ago, I asked a group of my Year 9 students to identify something they find very annoying or frustrating. Can you guess what they came up with? After the complaints about homework, of course, it was parents. More specifically, they all got annoyed by the "Parent Questions". The Parent Questions usually go something like this: "How was your day?", "What happened today?", "What did you learn?", and I bet as soon as you hear one of these questions, you just switch off, right?!

Let's get one thing straight from the very beginning here: everybody in your life has a certain role to play in your life. It is some people's job to be annoying, someone else's job to upset you, and someone else might have the role of encouraging you to see the funny side of things. Your parents are no different; it is their job to ask these questions, and as soon as we accept that, we can move on and deal with it.

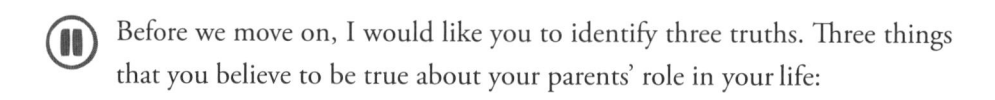

Before we move on, I would like you to identify three truths. Three things that you believe to be true about your parents' role in your life:

1.

2.

3.

Are the ones you have identified similar or different to the ones I've identified below?

1. **Your parents are doing the best job that they can.** Even though there are loads of parenting books out there, I've yet to meet one parent who is fully sure they are doing everything right, because quite frankly, I don't believe that even exists.
2. **Your parents are not perfect; no one is.** They will make mistakes, and they will make wrong choices because that's how we learn.
3. **It is their job to ask questions.** They are your parents, and they have a right to know what is going on with you, and your life.

Here's the big thing: if you don't tell them things or share information with them, then they will ask about it.

Once you accept these things, it gets easier right away.

▶ Remember the story about Jane in the last chapter? Well, it's very similar here. If you put the label "controlling" onto your parents then that is all you will see, and this makes for a very difficult relationship, full of confrontation and attempts at "winning". I want to encourage you now to think of a different way of seeing your parents. Think of words that are constructive to a healthy relationship:

Using this list of more helpful words from above, create your own list of truths regarding your parents, or simply extend the list from above. What do you believe to be true of them? What do they want for you? Again, this could be a great activity to do with a friend to help get someone else's perspective on things:

Okay, if it's the same twenty questions every day, what are you going to do about it? Aim to be part of the solution and not the problem! Please remember, I'm not here to side with your parents because I'm an adult. That's not how this works. Nor am I here to side with you just because I've written this book for you. It's about me providing an objective viewpoint. When you see your parents after your school day, what will you choose to do? What options do you have? Staring out the car window with your arms folded and mumbling "Fine" isn't really the most constructive choice, is it?

> Now, what kind of response is going to be most conducive to a positive and healthy relationship with your parents? Why?

My group of Year 9 students came up with some great ideas, and this was my favorite: "Miss, I know it's not about winning, but I'm going to get in there first. Before Mum has time to ask that one question of 'How was your day?', I'm going to ask her how her day was". I loved this and set the group this task for the weekend. When I saw the group the following week, and I asked them how it went, they all laughed at how shocked their parents were at being asked how their day was, instead of getting the usual silence or one-word answers!

> Take control of the situation yourself, and provide a solution to the problem you're facing by looking at the options you have. A choice is always better than no choice, and a person who is flexible in their approach to a problem will find the most solutions too. It might be weird at first if this is something you're not used to doing, but a lot of this book is about constructing new and better habits for yourself, and that includes how you interact with other people, including your parents. My students were laughing at their experiences over the weekend, and reconstructing the shocked or delighted looks on their parents' faces, when one student asked this great question: "But Miss, what do you do if you just don't feel like talking? I don't want to be rude to my dad and say that, but I feel it's wrong of me to pretend my day was fine if it really wasn't, you know?" This is a fantastic question; I loved it. Look at all the honesty, respect, and care shown in this one short sentence. Again, we looked at options. We knew it had to be something that was polite and honest, as the student had expressed not wanting to be rude, or to act as if her day was fine if it wasn't. So, this is what we came up with:

"Dad, to be honest, I had a bit of a mixed day and don't feel like talking about it right now. I'm going to sort some stuff out, and I might need your help later if that's okay."

or

"Dad, to be honest, it was an exhausting day with all those tests. I need some me time, and then I'll be fine."

There are a few common themes here, but the main point is all about communication. Communicate with your parents as best as you can. I fully understand that it's not always plain-sailing, but that's part of what this book is about, too: helping you communicate more effectively.

KEY TAKEAWAYS FROM THIS CHAPTER:

❶

Put yourself in your mum or dad's shoes. They want to know how your day was, they want to make sure you're okay, and they do this by asking questions. It's just one of the things they do to build a better relationship with you and show you they care and love you.

❷

If you don't like the questions you are being asked, then take control of the situation and change it. Go first and ask the questions when you see your parents instead. They'll really appreciate you making the effort.

❸

If you need some quiet time first before you have a chat about your day, then tell your parents that. The less you choose to communicate with them, the more questions they'll ask you!

"Good communication must be H.O.T. — meaning honest, open, and two-way."

DAN OSWALD

34 I feel like I'm compared to my siblings all the time and I hate it.

"Why can't you be more like your brother/sister?" Sound familiar? If you're an only child then you can probably move straight to the next chapter, unless comparisons are created between you and your cousins or friends, of course, then you'd better keep reading!

My instant reaction to this statement is three-fold and based on a search for evidence:

1. What happens to allow yourself to feel this way?
2. What makes you think they're better than you?
3. How are you never allowed to forget it?

Take these thoughts out of your head now and write them down so we can deal with them properly:

The first step here is to realize that you cannot control what other people say at all, but you can ALWAYS control YOUR REACTIONS to things. What are some better reactions you'd like to have in response to these words or actions?

Now, what stops you from having these reactions already?

And what would you need to have or do in order to have these better reactions? If you could wave a magic wand what resources would you ask for?

Remember, resources come in many different forms. It could be greater self-confidence, time, courage, greater self-esteem, the ability to forgive, the ability to forget, the ability to be assertive, or the ability speak up for yourself. Keep it positive. Many of the young people I work with say that they'd like the confidence to speak their minds to their parents about how these comparisons make them feel. I know this is where it can be easier to sweep it under the carpet rather than have an actual conversation, but when we don't deal with things they do come back to bite us in the backside.

⏸ Let's look at a few ways of dealing with this:

1. **Listen to the full story:**
   Before you go jumping into anything, always make sure you have the full, correct story. I've been guilty myself of picking up on one part of the conversation that perhaps resonates with how we are feeling at that time, and not listening to what else is being said. For example, if we're feeling a bit hostile towards someone, then that can encourage us only to hear the negative things they say about us or to only look at their negative behaviours instead of looking at the full picture. This is an example of all or nothing thinking from Chapter 2. Consider the following is said by your parents:

"We've become quite worried about your math results recently because Mrs. Ford says you've got the potential to be fantastic, but she feels you're just not working to your full potential right now. We're a bit concerned because even John has said you're not as attentive in the class."

Now, from this piece of the conversation, I think we'd all agree that it's expressing concern and worry. But sometimes we hear what we want, and we don't listen to the full message. If we're angry with our parents at a time when they deliver a message, we can take it up as an attack on us. Think about it and get a different perspective on the real situation:

Also, ask yourself if there is truth in there. Not one of us is perfect, and just because a message is delivered in a way we don't like doesn't mean it's false either. Be objective and look at the bigger picture. What do you see?

2. **Be more assertive.**
    Being assertive doesn't mean being aggressive, rather it's all about being heard. There are a few key components to it such as:
    - Use "I" statements/avoid "you" statements
    - Explain how you are feeling
    - Be very direct about the issue
    - State what you want
    - Offer a compromise

    Using the points above, construct a few sentences you could use to have an assertive conversation. I'll help you more with this below, but give it a go on your own first.

    Remember, keep it short and sweet so the meaning of your message doesn't get lost or confusing. It could go something like this:

    "**I feel** very hurt when I'm compared to John in terms of my achievement at school. **I feel** like I'm not good enough when these comparisons are made. **I'd like to** be recognized for my efforts, such as in art this term. **What would you like from me?**"

    It's short and sweet. The son/daughter has stated what they would like and is also offering to make some type of change to compromise. Remember change is a two-way street, so never expect someone to change without meeting them halfway.

3. **Look for the positive intention.**
    Every behaviour that people choose to carry out has some benefit for them—though not always for the other people involved, of course. Some people say or do things for power, pleasure, a sense of independence, maturity, whatever it may be. Can you think of a **positive** reason your parents would create such comparisons? What would they be hoping to achieve?

Looking for positive intentions can be tricky, so if you're stuck with this one think about it like this: Could these comparisons be their way of trying to motivate you to do more? Could it be that they see more potential in you, and they hope that by drawing comparisons that will ignite your motivation?

4. **Ask your parents what those positive intentions are and have a discussion about it.**
If we never ask, we never know, and instead we come up with our own ideas about what these comparisons mean, then off we go on the vicious mind-reading circle from Chapter 2 again. The next time a comparison is made, what could you say in reply to it? What are your options?

Yes, you could start screaming and shouting and slamming doors, but that's not very helpful communication. What's a better reaction? How about this:

"I know there's probably a positive reason for making these comparisons between John and me, but honestly, I don't see it. Can you explain it to me, because it's really hurtful to hear these comparisons, I feel like I'm not good enough".

Let's be very clear here, there is never anything wrong with admitting how you feel about something, whether you are male or female. Saying how you feel doesn't make you vulnerable to attack by others, rather it gives you strength because it's honest.

When have you planned to have this conversation?

If you've had this conversation, how did it go?

What worked well?

Is there anything you would have done differently?

KEY TAKEAWAYS FROM THIS CHAPTER:

❶

Just because you feel compared to your sibling doesn't mean that this is the case. Become aware of specific incidences that trigger these feelings within you and then you can do something about it. As with any of the thinking errors we have already looked at, it's important that you check for evidence based on facts.

❷

If you are being compared to someone else, ask yourself *How is this a problem for me?* Is it the comparison that is being made, or perhaps the person making the comparison? Use your answers to then address the situation in an assertive manner.

❸

Staying quiet about something that bothers you will never solve it, so speak assertively to the person creating the comparisons, being direct and taking responsibility for your feelings.

"No-one can make you feel inferior without your consent."

— ELEANOR ROOSEVELT

35 I'm leaving for university next year, but my parents still treat me like I'm twelve.

Ah yes, the "When will they treat me like an adult?" question. A couple of years ago I asked my coach trainers the very same question.

I said, "When I go home to visit my parents it's like I'm fourteen again. My dad has already made plans, he tells me what to do and who to see. When will this end?" At the time I hated my coach's response; I actually couldn't believe he asked it. But later it made a lot of sense.

He asked, "Well, do you act like you're fourteen again when you go home?" And immediately, I had one of those light bulb moments and thought, *Oh. My. God. I think I do!* It can be very easy for us to blame others for how we are treated, it's harder to look inwards and reflect on our own behaviour, but that is what self-awareness is all about. Instead of looking outside and at others as the source of the problem, let's learn to look inwards first. Yes, we're not always the source of the problem, but do we always act as the solution either?

So, here's my question to you: Do you still act like you are twelve? Are your parents reacting to your behaviour? Again, I'm not saying this is all your fault. I'm providing food for thought and an objective viewpoint—give it some thought. Sometimes we can say we feel like we're being treated in a certain way, but we know from looking at thinking errors in Chapter 2 that feelings aren't facts, so just because you feel this way, is it really the case? I felt like I was being treated like a teenager again when I returned home, and when I reflected on my behaviour I realized that I sometimes acted like a teenager again. Ergo, that's the response I'm going to get! But I also misread many signs, too. I felt that when my dad made plans for us without actually consulting me, that he was rude and presumptive when those aren't the facts at all. My Dad was trying to be inclusive and thought the plans he made would be a nice way for us to spend time together, which they were. Feelings are not facts.

⏸ Take a few minutes now before we go any further to look at the facts that are present in your situation. It's always a good idea to look at things from your parents' perspective too, so take yourself to an objective place in the house, or outside, and really put yourself in their shoes. Now look at the reasons your parents are choosing particular behaviours with you, What are they?

You could also use a Helicopter View, too. Imagine you have a completely objective role, like you're a reporter or something. I want you to imagine you are flying above your house during a particular time when it feels like you are being treated like a twelve-year-old. Now, from this objective, impartial position, what do you notice about how the people below are acting?

You:

Mum/Dad or both:

How does this Helicopter View help you to see things differently already? What's different?

If you feel you're still in the same position, let's look at how we can move forward. Identify, very clearly, how you want your parents to treat you. For example, do you want to be given more freedom? Do you want to be allowed out at weekends? Would you like them to trust you more? Be very specific about what you want and how you want to be treated:

▶ Now to change the response you get from your parents, you need to make some changes first, because if you keep doing what you've always done, then you'll keep getting the same response. I want you to think of three things you can stop doing. Three things you need to stop doing to take you closer to your goal. Could it be that you need to stop answering back when they ask you to do something? Do you need to stop disrespecting the freedom you currently have? Think of things you currently say or do, which you are determined to change:

1.

2.

3.

Now think of three things that you will start doing. Three things that show you are the type of person you want your parents to see you as. Could you take more initiative and do something before you have to be asked to do it? Could you earn some of your own money? Do you need to respect boundaries set by your parents more? Could you communicate with them more? Again, these could be based on things you say or things you do.

1.

2.

3.

If you're only bringing 50 percent of yourself to a relationship, then don't be surprised if you only get 50 percent out of it. Bring 100 percent of yourself to the relationships that matter the most to you, and you will see the difference this makes. What do you do if nothing changes and you still feel like you're being treated like you're twelve? Firstly, make sure that you are putting 100 percent into the relationship, and evaluate the changes you've made so far. What have you changed?

How long has it been since you made these changes?

Have you been consistent with your new actions?

⏸ If you feel happy enough with the changes you've made, that's great! If things still haven't changed then, you guessed it: it's time for a conversation with your parents! The benefits of communicating with your parents are huge. Remember it's not about winning or always getting your way, it's about being heard. Could it be that they have absolutely no idea that you are feeling like this at all? Remember they're not mind readers; none of us are. Talk to them about this using the guidelines about being assertive from the last chapter. A key component in this type of conversation is compromise. If you want something from them, then be prepared to meet them halfway. If you're worried about the conversation and how to go about it, use the space below to help structure your ideas:

1. Use "I" statements
2. State how you feel
3. Be direct about what you would like/want
4. Avoid "you" statements
5. Offer a compromise

I feel   when
I would like
How about we agree to/Could we agree that

Feel free to write your own one:

Before this conversation takes place, is there anything you need to do? Anything you need to have to deliver this message as best as you can?

Remember you begin to build a solid foundation for any relationship when you use open and honest communication. Well done for taking this step. I know it's not easy, so give yourself a pat on the back.

KEY TAKEAWAYS FROM THIS CHAPTER:

❶

You've always more chance of being treated like an adult if you act like one, so the first step is to become aware of your own behaviour, especially in the company of your parents. If you go around slamming doors and swearing when you don't get your own way, then don't be surprised when this childlike behaviour gets a childlike response.

❷

Your parents might have actually no idea this is how they treat you. When you raise the issue with them, make sure to give them clear and specific examples of how or when you feel treated like a child—never expect them to simply know.

❸

Have a solution-focused conversation instead of one which seeks to point fingers and place blame on others, being clear about what being treated like an adult means to you.

"If you want to know if a person will change, don't listen to their words, but watch their behavior."

— MARILOU SEAVEY

36 My parents don't allow me to go out and all my friends are allowed out.

"But EVERYONE is going, and I'm the only one not going!" Sound familiar? If so, read on. Knowing that your friends and peers have certain freedoms that you don't can be really rubbish, full stop. So, if you want to go to a friend's party and your parents won't allow you to go, what are your options?

1. Sneak out and go anyway. Who cares?
2. Continue to beg and plead thinking they'll eventually give in. You can break them!
3. Respect your parents' decision knowing they have your best interest at heart.

Which did you choose? Which one will lead to the better home relationship? Which one builds trust? I'd love to know the answers you're saying in your head right now! How about if I told you this:

> Your parents aren't the fun police in disguise. Their goal in life is not to make you miserable. As hard as this may be to accept right now, they do feel they are doing the right thing by not letting you go. What we probably don't know as teenagers is that a lot of parents are worried. They are petrified, in fact. They have been dreading the day you come to them and say you want to go to a party, or you want to go on a date, or to a club. They are worried because of many things. They are terrified there'll be alcohol at the party, and even if you don't drink, they are terrified in case someone spikes your drink. They are worried about drugs, and again, it's not that they don't trust you, but maybe they don't trust some of your friends, and maybe they have very good reason for this, too. Or maybe they don't have a good reason not to trust your friends—we're all guilty of judging people when we shouldn't. If you're a girl, your parents are terrified you'll meet the wrong guy, and worst-case scenario, that you'll be assaulted. Unfortunately, it's not all plain-sailing for guys either because it's not only young girls who

are victims of assault, young men are at risk, too. And the list goes on. Do you want to know what it's like inside the mind of a parent? You've either got to be one, or speak to many of them, and thankfully, I've done the latter. I know you'll probably sit there and say they can't keep you wrapped up in cotton wool until you're out of the house either, but until you're eighteen, they can! That's not to say that if your parents allow you certain freedoms, then they just don't care about you. Parents come to parenting with many different views and perspectives, but whatever their journey through parenthood may be, you can guarantee one thing—they're looking out for you.

For many parents, the problem is that they know what they were doing at your age! They now have the benefit of hindsight, and hence they try to protect you from making the same mistakes they did, with partying, experimentation, relationships, whatever it is. I never thought I would hear myself say this, but I do see now that my parents were right. Oh, it's still horrible to actually admit it!

And I don't think I'm ready to tell them that myself, though. My mum was right about so many things and so was my dad. It's like they knew it was going to happen, and I guess they did, because it happened to them or because they saw it happen to others.

▶ So, what do you do?

Well, this depends on your choice of 1, 2, or 3 above! If you sneaked out of the house, then that's a different conversation, because trust has been broken and it's not going to come back on a whim. There are always consequences to actions in life. If you have broken your parents' trust, and they still let you go out, then once again that's another conversation to have. But what do you do if you're the best son/daughter you can be, you're doing your best to adhere to your mum and dad's rules and respect them, but you still want that little bit of freedom? What do you do then? Is it going to come as any surprise to you that I'm going to suggest a conversation or form of communication? Of course not! I'm all about improving relationships. Communication, like trust, is a foundation to any relationship. Even though I listed a range of worries some parents have, this is not to say these are the worries of YOUR parents. How would it be if you actually asked what your parents' worries were? Not a "Why won't you let me go?" confrontation, but more of a "Can you help me see it from your point of view please, because I don't understand it?" conversation.

Before you enter into that conversation and ask that question, ask yourself what your outcome is? What do you want to get from the conversation? And if it's to understand where your parents are coming from and what their position is, then you're on the right track. Enter into a conversation to win, and you've gone in with the wrong attitude completely. It's not about winning here and being allowed to go to the party. It's about being heard. (Anyone keeping count of how many times I've said this phrase so far?) There is also no guarantee that your parents will actually tell you why they won't let you go, and that's something you'll have to accept. I'll mention it in my Guide for Parents, don't worry!

▶ Write down the outcome you want from having this conversation with your parents:

⏸ If your parents do share their concerns with you, again, respect them. Laugh in their faces, and you're not going out for a VERY long time! You want them to respect your opinions and values, then show respect for theirs, too. Meet people halfway, remember. In respecting their concerns, how can you move forward? What kind of compromises can you make? Is it about time? The people you'll be with? The location you want to go to? Other parents?

Are there things about your own behaviour you can alter to build more trust in the relationship? For example, if you know that your parents want you to communicate with them more when you are out, can you make sure you message them when you arrive, and when you leave the event? Set an alarm if you have to.

Are there things about the situation you need to adapt to, like making some greater compromises and be home earlier than you want to? For example, if your parents want you home by 10 p.m., are you taking liberties by coming home at 10:30 p.m.? You'd like them to be on time picking you up, so do the same for them. Give respect and you'll get respect.

Are there things you need to simply accept about your parents and their attitudes to nights out?

222 • PRESS PLAY

On a final note in this chapter, here's my personal advice—don't lie to your parents. You might think they're ancient and haven't got a clue, but keep in mind that they've known you forever! Yes, there are times when they might choose to see what they want to, but they also know when you're trying to pull the wool over their eyes. Get found out lying to them and believe me, it'll take you a lot longer to build up that foundation of trust again. If you do get found out lying to them, then just face the facts, don't dig yourself deeper!

KEY TAKEAWAYS FROM THIS CHAPTER:

❶

Your parents are not fun sponges and they're not trying to make you miserable; they are always trying to protect you and they're probably also very concerned about letting you out because they know exactly what they were doing at your age, too. Speak to your parents in a calm and polite manner to find out what it is that concerns them about you going out.

❷

If it's a question of trust, then you have got to do the work to show them that they can trust you. Like most parents they'll want to see they can trust you through the behaviour that you choose not what you tell them you will or won't do.

❸

Know that if you make a promise to them about a time that you'll be home or something that you won't get involved in, you need to be willing to keep that promise, because if you break that trust it will take you a lot longer to get it back.

"You are free to choose, but you are not free to alter the consequences of your decisions."

EZRA TAFT BENSON

37. My parents keep asking me what I'm going to do after school and I have no idea.

If you could do anything at all with your life after school what would it be?

If you had the opportunity to study anything at all in college/university, what would it be?

What are you great at?

I deliver assemblies to schools and seminars to companies on stress management. One of the slides I used recently in schools is on this very issue. When I asked the audience of about two hundred Year 12 and 13 students how many of them knew at this very point in time what they wanted to study when they left school, about twenty hands went up. Then I asked how many of them had some idea, and a few more hands went up. And when I asked how many had no idea at all, guess what happened? The majority of hands went up. All of the students turned to see who had raised their hands, and then laughed at the fact so many of them had! If you feel like you have no idea at all what you want to do after school, you're not alone.

▶ But where do you even begin?

STEP 1: Know and accept that at the age of sixteen, seventeen, eighteen, nineteen—or any age, really—you are NOT expected to know what you want to do for the rest of your life. FACT. But that's the way we think about it, isn't it? We often think that we have to have the same job or occupation for the rest of our working lives. Why do we sometimes think the choices we make now are it and there's no going back? Newsflash! It's not about going back, it's always about moving forward, and sometimes in life, you will decide to take different routes and different paths. If we use a road trip analogy here of getting to where we want to go, sometimes you might decide to stop and rest on the road trip. You might decide to pick up a passenger or decide you need a new vehicle. You might ditch the passenger, or decide to take the long scenic drive instead of the motorway. You get where this is going, don't you? Even if you decided to make a quick trip back home while on your journey, it's never about going backwards.

STEP 2: Know that it's okay to change your mind. You don't have to stay on that same road forever. So, if you now accept that it's okay to change your mind, how does that help take you closer to choosing a college course/a career?

STEP 3: Whatever you are going to put time and effort into must meet your values. You cannot expect yourself to get excited about a course or job that doesn't respect your values. Here's that question again, what do you value in life? What's important to you in life? Identify at least three things and keep asking yourself this question again and again until you get to the bottom line: your core values, or the things that mean the most to you. It's always useful to have a friend ask you the questions, but feel free to give it a go yourself.

What's important to me in life?

What's important about this in particular?

What's important about that?

And what's important about that?

Keep asking yourself this question until you get to that bottom line. Once you have an idea of the things that are important to you, you're off to a flying start. Too many of us end up doing things that often don't meet our values, and this is never going to sit well with you. Knowing your values and doing right by them is key. Sometimes we get a negative gut reaction when one of our values is violated.

▶ Keeping your values in mind, what kinds of jobs or courses might be relevant? Yes, this might involve a little research, but remember to be resourceful. You're not expected to have all the answers, so let's ask ourselves better questions like:

1. Who do I know that can help me find out this information?
2. Who do I know currently in this line of work?
3. Where can I find out more information?

When you've got more information, you're in a much better place to make more informed decisions. If none of the jobs or careers you come up with interest you, then it could be that you've skimmed over the work on your values, and maybe you need to spend a bit more time considering what's really important to you. Keep in mind that it's important to do what you *want* to do, and not what you think you *should* do, as we mentioned in the early chapter. Yes, your parents might think you should study chemistry, but what do you want to do?

STEP 4: Work to your strengths. We all have areas that we'd like to improve on, and I'm not advising you to ignore any weaknesses and never ask for help in those areas, but I am saying to find out what your strengths are first and work towards those. Not only does working on your strengths seem "easier" but it can also motivate us as we will look forward to that activity more than something we're not great at.

Working towards what you are good at doesn't even feel like work, because it's something you enjoy. It's also something you already know you can do, which makes it easier! How many people do you know who are fully aware of what their strengths are? Too often we're unaware of where our real strengths lie. We're told by our parents and teachers we're great at this and that, and I'm not accusing them of lying here, but I bet there are things that you are *even better* at? Things that you do that you might take for granted, like being an excellent communicator, or bringing people together, listening, or problem-solving.

In a recent assembly I held, one of the slides read, "It's not okay to change your mind". As soon as it popped up on the screen, I could see all the faces, teachers included, develop puzzled and perplexed looks, as if to say, "What the hell?" I started chuckling, because when I asked, "Well, this is what we all think, isn't it?", they all agreed. I went on to tell them briefly about my own career path. Actually, path is the wrong word completely. I think if my mum could describe it, it might be more of a "career jungle without any path". It started when I was very young and it went a bit like this:

I want to be an international showjumper. Yes, I love horses, that's what I want. Then after a few years, when I realize riding horses is a lot of hard work, I thought, *Oh, acting, how I love acting, maybe I'll do theatre studies, move to Hollywood, and win an Oscar!* A few months later it was *No, I love the horses too much, so I'm going to have my own equestrian center.* Career decided. Until my fifth year of school, where I was saying, *Oh, hello law! Let's study you and change the world while making millions at the same time.* Fast-forward to the end of my first year in my new school for Sixth Form, and I was then thinking *Yes, definitely psychology, that's what I was born to do. In fact, psychoanalytic studies. Oh wait, how much did you say it costs? Right, okay, back to the horses or the psychology?*

This went on and on until it was time to choose a university with my exam results, but then I didn't make the grade for psychology in Trinity College, so I had to go back to the drawing board! I realised I could try to get into psychology via Arts in Galway, so I started a degree there. All was going well until my brain started ticking again in my final year and I heard myself saying, *Oh, how about I apply for the Irish Army to get into the Equitation School? Oh yes, please! No, I'll head off travelling.* And I did, I headed off on an around the world adventure for six months. Meanwhile, I had applied for my higher diploma in Education, but forgotten about it, until I got offered a place on the course in Dublin. *Looks like I'm doing teaching then.*

And in true Linda fashion, after a few years in the classroom, I thought, *But wait, what about my own equestrian center? Or my own PR company? Yes! Let's do another course on public relations while I'm doing supply teaching, oh amazing!* Turns out that I wasn't ready to jump in and set up my own PR company at the time and supply teaching wasn't giving me the financial security I needed to live comfortably in Dublin. There were no full-time history teaching positions available at the time either, so when a job came up in the Middle East I thought, *Sure, why not! I'm not doing anything else. One year done, will I stay another year? Yes, why not! And another? Yes. How about ten? Sure!* Which is how I ended up living in Dubai married to Steve.

Fast-forward a few years later, I discovered NLP Coaching and fell in love with it straight away. After that whirlwind romance, I realised it was something I wanted to invest in long-term and thought, *Maybe I can have my own business with this? Let's give it a go!* And here I am.

I've lost count of how many times I changed my mind about my chosen career. In the midst of all that mind-changing, did you notice any key themes that kept popping up, something all the career paths had in common? One of my key themes is that I've always loved making things better. I've always wanted to improve things, to make a difference. Like with my horse-riding. When I exercised and competed with other people's horses, I did so to improve them. When I thought about law, I thought I could improve people's lives and their situations. With the acting idea, I thought I could make a difference through entertaining people. With teaching, I knew I was making a difference and improving people's lives, and now that's the same with my coaching. I know I'm making a difference, I know I'm giving people the tools to improve. But there's also another value there, too: independence. I've always been very independent and sometimes to my own detriment. But if you look at those careers, a lot of them had a focus of it being "my own thing": the equestrian center, the PR company, and now my own coaching business. I know that when I'm not working to improve something or when I don't feel independent, I'm not very happy in what I'm doing.

So, what makes you happy?

What are you happiest doing?

And what are you great at?

KEY TAKEAWAYS FROM THIS CHAPTER:

❶

When thinking about a career, one of the most important factors is to choose something that you're interested in. It's your life, your career or your job, so it's important that you're happy with it. Start by asking yourself what's important to you in a career. What are you interested in? What are you good at?

❷

Carry out research and look at various career paths to jobs you're interested in, asking yourself where you are in terms of these paths right now. For example, do you have the specific subject set required for further study in this area?

❸

Carrying out a SWOT (Strengths, Weaknesses, Opportunities, and Threats) analysis of careers you're interested in can also be really helpful. It works even better if you are able to speak to people currently working in those professions.

> "Success is achieved by developing our strengths, not by eliminating our weaknesses."
>
> — MARILYN VOS SAVANT

38 I feel like I'm not being true to myself or true to my family, and it eats me up inside.

I don't know many people who like dealing with conflict, because it usually makes us feel very uneasy. And when it's an internal conflict with ourselves, it can literally feel like something is eating you up inside. As a result, many of us will put off dealing with conflict head on. Some of us will just try to avoid it, some of us will try to supress it within us, or some of us might try to pretend it's not even happening. We do these things in order to try to protect ourselves, but in the long run they don't help us and actually stop us moving forward.

What is inner conflict?

Inner conflict is an internal battle with yourself, usually between something you want to do and something else that you feel you "should" do. People might describe inner or personal conflict as "two parts of themselves" that often want "two different things". For example, there might be the part of you that knows it's good for you to study and the part of you that wants to play video games instead. This example of studying versus playing video games isn't a huge issue compared to when someone feels they are not being true to themselves—this is trickier because it goes deeper.

Dealing with deeper inner conflict can feel like you're being pulled in two different directions: where you're trying to stay true to your own values while also attempting to satisfy someone else, with different values or beliefs, at the same time. The student who told me he felt he wasn't being true to himself feels like he is having to change himself in order to fit in or be the kind of person other people want him to be. Imagine how horrible this must be, to feel like you cannot be your true self, to feel like you have to hide a part of you.

⏸ How do you recognise inner conflict?

You'll recognise it because something just won't feel right, maybe like a part of you is out of sync with the rest of you. You might feel discomfort, stress or even pain, and this is why we need to deal with the conflict and not ignore it. Where people experience confusion over gender or sexual orientation, for example, they can face great internal conflict as they battle against who they feel they should be (according to family or cultural values or beliefs) compared to who they really are.

▶ **What can you do about it?**

It's very important not to ignore or suppress this feeling. You have to do your best to get the conflict out of your head where you can deal with it rationally. Take some time to investigate any discomfort experienced and try to find its source. Give the following questions a go to help you:

1. Where is this conflict coming from?

2. What thoughts and feelings are associated with it?

3. What, if any, behaviours are associated with the conflict experienced?

4. What's an example of you not being true to yourself in this situation?

5. How or where are you not being true to your family?

6. What would happen if you were true to yourself and/or your family?

7. What stops you from being true to yourself and/or your family?

Remember that fear is only helpful in certain situations to protect you or get you away from danger; it's not a helpful feeling here. And feelings like guilt and shame don't deserve a place in your fantastic life.

8. Who would you be if you didn't have this inner conflict?

⏸ Your family and real friends will love you no matter what you tell them. Yes, it might be difficult for them to hear certain things at first, especially if what you tell them is very different to their own beliefs—we all like our values and beliefs to be respected. If your friends find it impossible to accept what you tell them about yourself, then perhaps they were friends who weren't meant to stay in your life, and that's okay. The fact that you are now being 100 percent honest with yourself, having resolved that conflict, will give you a newfound sense of confidence allowing you to gravitate towards people who will love you for who you are: YOU.

KEY TAKEAWAYS FROM THIS CHAPTER:

❶

Inner conflict is a struggle with ourselves; a struggle between what we feel we *should* do and how we stay true to ourselves. Unfortunately, many of us choose to suppress inner conflict rather than deal with it in a rational way. Consistently ignoring our true values will only lead to further discomfort.

❷

Write it out. The very act of unloading the upsetting emotions onto paper will help you begin to deal with the conflict. You could then go one step further and write out your next step to deal with it.

❸

A major cause of internal conflict is the constant violation of our own values. To resolve this conflict, make sure that you are staying true to your values and not trying to satisfy someone else's.

"Today you are you, that is truer than true. There is no one alive who is youer than you."

— DR. SEUSS

39) I'm fed up living away from my real home. We get shipped around a lot with my parents' work.

I think it's challenging enough being a young person nowadays, as you try to figure out your place in the world, and I can only imagine that not residing in your country of birth, your home country, makes this a little more challenging. Throw something into this mix, like a parent's career which involves a lot of travel or a lot of moving around, and that's a great recipe for some very interesting situations and conversations!

> Two things are going on here. Firstly, the fact that this person is fed up of living away from their real home, and secondly, the fact that they must move with their parents' jobs. First of all, if you're in this situation, then I'm not going to pretend that I know what it's like to move from one country to another. I grew up in Ireland, I stayed there until I was twenty-one, and then moved to the Middle East, Qatar to be precise. I have travelled around the world, but I've been lucky in that it's all been on my own terms, it's been my own choice. Of course, I miss my home. I miss my family, friends, and Ireland in general, but I also know that I've a better opportunity here at the moment to build my business. There are many things I do to keep my "Irishness" alive. If you are a young person who is living abroad, and maybe a bit fed up of it at the moment or missing home a bit more than usual, what are some things you can do or organize to keep your own culture alive? Write down five to start with.

1.

2.

3.

4.

5.

For each of these five things, identify a step you could take **today** to get the ball rolling:

1.

2.

3.

4.

5.

Now, for the young people I've spoken to about this specific issue, the element of choice seems to play a huge role in the frustration and anger that sometimes comes about as a result of this constant moving. Often you feel like you have no choice. So now, how about we work on identifying and creating some choice? While I can't relate to the moving around with your family very well, I can fully relate to the idea and desire for choice in our lives. If you've already completed

Part 1 of the book, then you'll probably already have an idea of your core values, or at least the things that are most important to you in your life. If choice is one of these, then this might be something that is particularly affecting you. As with any issue, a great place to start is to look at the things you can control about the situation compared to the things that you cannot.

Situation:	
Things I can control about this situation:	**Things I cannot control about it:**

If you are feeling stuck with this part, it may be because, at this very moment in time, there doesn't really seem to be anything that you can control about this situation. However, I promise you there is. Give the exercise another go. It will also help to look at and write down some things that perhaps you need to accept about the situation. When we accept certain things instead of fighting them, that's us taking control, and we love being in control of things.

⏸ Identify three things that, when you accept them about this situation, will help you deal with it in a more constructive way:

1.

2.

3.

Accepting things about life can be easier said than done. Is there anything you would need to accept these things? This could be anything from a conversation with your parents about their work, to joining a new club of some kind to meet new people. You know what it's like when you focus on the negative aspects of something? Yes, more negative things pop up. It's like a negative thought cycle that just produces more of the same kind of thoughts. If you're allowing yourself time to focus on the negative aspects of where you are living at the moment, then that's ALL you are going to see about it. It's like wearing a particular pair of glasses which focus on the negatives. What can you do instead? Well, when it comes to your thoughts, you've always got a choice. Work on changing your thoughts so that they serve you better or carry on with the same negative thoughts and see how that helps you! Take yourself through the steps below to investigate where you can begin to make changes. I've given you some examples to help you start. These might be similar or completely different to your situation.

STEP 1: How does thinking negatively about the current situation help you? Who does it help?

>**Example:** *I know it doesn't help me, but I don't know how to change it either.*

STEP 2: What would you need to *think* differently about the current situation?

>**Example:** *I'd need a new perspective on the situation I'm currently in on where we're living right now, almost like a new mindset.*

STEP 3: For some people, it's about *feeling* differently about where they live. What would help you feel differently about where you currently live?

>**Example:** *I'm avoiding the fact that I'm quite lonely here. I don't feel like I've got close friends here, compared to where we lived before. If I had closer friends, I think I'd feel better about the situation.*

STEP 4: Identify three things that you enjoy about where you live:

Example: *I'm in a really good school, so I know I'm really lucky there, we get to spend every weekend outside doing something different. Travelling around on my own is easy.*

STEP 5: Highlight at least three things you enjoy that you can do in your current country of residence that you could not do in your home country:

STEP 6: As a young person, what opportunities does your current country of residence offer you?

STEP 7: As a family, what does living in this country provide your family with? Consider each family member, and ask them personally about this, so you have their own words and perspectives. No mind-reading!

STEP 8: Having investigated the opportunities and perks of where you currently live from different perspectives, how does this change how you feel about it now?

STEP 9: It can be easy to fall into our old way of thinking, and back into a fixed mindset, so what can you do to remind yourself of the positives?

KEY TAKEAWAYS FROM THIS CHAPTER:

❶

It's not realistic to be a ray of sunshine all the time, but complaining about something will never make it better and will only highlight the negatives. The more you focus on the negatives, the more you'll see.

❷

Relocating isn't just stressful for you, it can be incredibly stressful for your parents and siblings, too. Share your concerns with your parents, ask them how they're coping with it or how they've coped with moving in the past.

❸

Labelling situations with "no choice" is not helpful and encourages us to play the victim role instead of taking control. Look at all the choices about the situation which you have, like how you respond and react to things, and use these to feel empowered.

"It's not just about developing an attitude of gratitude, but it's about actively practicing one; we can never expect to get more in our lives unless we are grateful for what we already have."

LINDA BONNAR

40 I'm worried my parents are going to get divorced.

When I read issues like this, and I don't know the full story, it's very hard for me to reply, "Your parents won't get divorced; everything will be okay". Because a) I CANNOT promise you that your parents won't get divorced, and b) as a coach, if I'm not honest with people then I'm not doing my job properly either.

And yes, I encourage people to be optimistic, but I also encourage them to be realistic.

Let's be realistic here first.

It's all about them: The fact that you have dramatically improved your behaviour or practiced guitar more or finally decided on that college place isn't going to change how your parents feel about each other. From the beginning, remember that any divorce or separation or changes in a marriage are not about you, it's all about your parents.

It's not your fault: Major changes in a marriage don't take place because of teenagers. Sure, there might be disagreements between a mother and father over how they deal with situations, but that's different. The desire for a separation or divorce comes from something much, much deeper. There could be arguments, frustrations, communication issues, perhaps relationships outside of the marriage have developed, but these are the issues regarding the marriage itself.

Knowing the reason doesn't mean YOU can fix it: Even if your parents told you the reasons for their divorce or separation, it doesn't mean you can fix it, and I know that's very hard to hear and accept. I know students who have tried to help their parents see each other in a new light, by organizing romantic meals or nights away, and so on. These are beautiful gestures, and I'm not saying they don't work, but at the end of the day, it is up to your parents to make the changes they need to make if the marriage is going to work. It's not the job of a teenager.

If in doubt, check it out: If you are worried about something, then the best thing for you to do is always to ask. If you were unsure about the date of an exam, what would you do? If you were worried about the steps to take in applying for college, what would you do? Of course, you'd ask. So, if something like your parents' marriage is worrying you, what are you going to do? Yes, ask. Speak to your parents. Tell them what you've seen, heard, and felt recently. What have those things led you to think or believe? It could be that your parents have a lot on their plates right now, and have been a bit stressed or on edge recently. By bringing it up, you're highlighting it to them, too, because perhaps they haven't been very conscious of how they've been communicating or acting in front of their children either. Sometimes nothing even has to be said, but you can feel the tension or the uneasiness around others, and if that's how you feel then say it.

Relationships have rough patches: We're all human, and sometimes we just want different things or have different perspectives on things. When this happens, relationships can go through rough patches. It is perfectly normal for people to express their needs and desires in various forms, and unfortunately these can take the form of unpleasant arguments between parents. You know what it's like when people are trying to come to a compromise and keep everyone happy? Sometimes a win-win situation is created and sometimes it's not. When we accept that relationships aren't perfect and we've got to do a bit of work on them, then it seems more manageable for us to work together and create that compromise. However, just remember that not everyone wants to compromise.

Naturally, of course, I'm hoping that you're the one who's put three and three together and got seventy-eight million and that your parents are just going through a rough patch.

▶ In the meantime, what can you do?

Talk about it: Confide in a friend, school counsellor, a family friend, or a teacher you trust, and talk to them about what you're experiencing. If your parents have chosen to get divorced then it's natural for you to feel angry, upset, frustrated, guilty and so on, but do not think for one second that you have to deal with this on your own.

Talk to your parents: Speak to them about what you're experiencing. Don't worry about putting extra pressure on them, because bringing these things into the open is much better for your mental health than keeping them locked up inside you.

Get support: You might find that talking about it is good, but you need something more. So, who can you ask for more support? What kind of support do you need?

Accept that it is not your fault: As we said above, changing your grades won't prevent this, and neither will be getting rid of your boyfriend or girlfriend that your parents don't like. It won't work because these things are not the reasons the divorce taking place. It may be that you need professional support as you deal with this, and that's fine.

Keep your routine going: Change is inevitable, we all know and accept that, so if there is a lot of change going on at home, then do your best to keep to your routine as much as possible. That way you've got some element of control. Keep your after-school activities going, keep up your sports training, and keep to plans with your friends.

KEY TAKEAWAYS FROM THIS CHAPTER:

❶

Every relationship and marriage has its ups and downs. If your parents have decided to get divorced, you must know that it is nothing you have done and nothing you can change. You may feel guilty, upset or frustrated but the decisions that a married couple make to get divorced are theirs.

❷

Make sure that you are talking to someone about the experience and know that you are never alone in what you're going through.

❸

Do your very best to recognise your strengths in terms of how you're coping with the divorce. Perhaps, you've noticed that you're much calmer when dealing with younger siblings or even other people as a result of what's going on at home.

"We cannot always control everything that happens to us in this life, but we can control how we respond."

L. LIONEL KENDRICK

Epilogue

And so there it is! I hope you've found this book helpful. Now you've even more powerful skills, tools and techniques to help you overcome challenges successfully and move forward confidently in your life. It's time to Press Play!

I want to thank you. I have loved writing this book for you and found the whole experience very cathartic, but I must admit, stressful at times too. It wasn't always easy, especially when the voice of self-doubt would creep in and spark the hamster wheel of questions going around and around in my head: *Why are you writing this anyway? What makes you think teenagers will be interested?* But that's when I had to practice what I preach. When these questions popped into my head, I had to be ready to fight them off. I had to check for evidence and dig deep to find my own self-confidence. I had to be willing to acknowledge the negative thoughts, and then replace them with more constructive thoughts, and you know what? When you do it consistently, it works. Please give it a try. You deserve the very best, and to not be held back by any Limiting Beliefs.

I'm also aware that making any kind of change in your life is easier said than done. But if you want to get different results in your life and you want to change your current situation, then you've got to make those changes. Be responsible for making those changes, take control of your life, and Press Play on a fresh start today.

I'm in the middle of putting my next coaching book together and always welcome your ideas, so please feel free to email me at linda@lindabonnarcoaching.com. Also join me and thousands of others in my open Facebook group, Linda Bonnar Life Coaching, where I post daily motivational and encouraging posts. You can also follow me on Instagram @lindabonnar_lifecoach and on Twitter @LBLifeCoach.

Notes

Part 1

PG. 21: Beck, A.T. (1976). *Cognitive Therapies and Emotional Disorders*. New York: New American Library.

Burns, D. D. (1980). *Feeling Good: The New Mood Therapy*. New York: New American Library.

PG. 45: Image of Balance Wheel from happilyinbalance.com.

PG. 71: Elevator Breathing Script, adapted from E. Gregory's mindfulness elevator breathing.

PG. 83: Peters, S. (2012). *The Chimp Paradox*. London: Vermilion.

Part 2

PG. 87: youngminds.co.uk

psychologytoday.com.

PG. 87: rcpsych.co.uk.

PG. 95: Goleman, D. (1995). *Emotional Intelligence*. New York: Bantam Books

Part 3

PG. 123: Carey, B. (2015). *How We Learn*. New York: Random House

PG. 134: www.businessinsider.com.au/the-15-richest-people-without-college-degrees-2010-11

PG. 184: stompoutbullying.org

Extras

Buttons: stevepaint/123RF

Acknowledgements

People provide support to us in so many different shapes and forms, and I really believe that no project is completed successfully alone. I would like to thank the following people for their continued support in helping me complete *Press Play*:

My amazing husband, Steve. Thank you for putting up with me and for making me laugh every single day; I'm the luckiest girl in the world!

I thank Kira at The Dreamwork Collective for her unwavering support, guidance, faith, love and encouragement in making my dream of this book a reality. Thank you also to Thalia at The Dreamwork Collective for believing in my book and seeing its value to young people.

Ema, for her relentless support and optimism, and for just being awesome! Jacqui, for being an absolute lady to aspire to be in life, for always being there and never judging. Claire, for her continued support in my business ventures and for her beautiful words. Yasmine, for her level-headedness, friendship, support and honesty. Aideen, for the years of love and laughter, for always knowing I had to learn my own lessons and for trusting me to do so.

To Marilou and Jerry Seavey, for helping me move forward in my own life and empowering me to become the best version of myself. And I thank everyone who contributed and discussed the real-life issues young people face with me. I simply could not have written this book without your help, your honesty, and your support. Your sincerity means the world to me and I'm incredibly grateful.

Thank you all, from the bottom of my heart.

About the Author

Linda spends her time working with amazing people and thinking of ways to bring a little more sparkle to the world. She used to be a high school history teacher, and now, thousands of hours of training and advanced NLP qualifications later, has her own thriving coaching business.

Linda has a slight obsession with running and tortoises, despite the fact that two don't often go together. She loves a good chat, a great laugh, and an even better sale!

Having overcome her own challenges with mental illness, Linda is a huge advocate of working to break the stigma and silence that surrounds the topic. To find out more about Linda and the work that she does, please visit her website lindabonnar.com.

About the Publisher

THE DREAMWORK COLLECTIVE

The Dreamwork Collective is an independent print and digital publishing house based in the Middle East. We are committed to sharing under-represented voices and untold stories from the Middle East with the entire world.

Our collective is filled with inspiring, creative and positive voices. Our authors write about all sorts of different topics but are united in their vision in wanting to make the world a better place.

Learn more about us here: thedreamworkcollective.com